Lynn –
Hope you enjoy this
book as much as
we did.
            Love,
            Phyg & Margie

Sled Dog Trails

Sled Dog Trails

Mary Shields
Illustrated by Nancy van Veenen

pyrola publishing

ACKNOWLEDGEMENTS

The following publishers, authors have generously given permission to use extended quotations from their works: Dodd, Mead and Company, Inc. for "The Spell of the Yukon" and "Call of the Wild" from *Collected Poems of Robert Service*, 1968; G.P. Putnam's Sons for *Across Arctic America, Narrative of the Fifth Thule Expedition,* by Knud Rasmussen, 1927; John Haines for material originally published in *Winter News* by Wesleyan University Press, 1966; Evelyn Heller for material written by her husband, Herbert Heller, in *Sourdough Sagas,* A Comstock Edition, 1967; and Sue Carrel for her previously unpublished poem. Material from *The ALASKA ALMANAC®* concerning the Iditarod race was originally published in the 1983 edition.

A thank you to all who helped, inspired, encouraged, shared and criticized:
Rich Barnes, Jean Chapman, Byron Fish, Tim Jones, Chuck Keim, John Manthei, Willard Manthei, Mardy Murie, Pat Oakes, Nancy van Veenen, Kathy Valentine, and my mom, Leah Shields.

Mary Shields
September 1983
College, Alaska

Library of Congress cataloging in publication data:
Shields, Mary.
  Sled dog trails.
  1. Sled dog racing—Alaska. 2. Dogsledding—Alaska.
3. Shields, Mary. I. Title.
SF440.15.S55 1984   798'.8   83-27548
ISBN 0-88240-258-7   Seventeenth Printing 2010

Designer: Jon.Hersh
Cover photo of Mary Shields by Evelyn Trabant
Printed in U.S.A.

pyrola publishing

p.o. box 80961 fairbanks alaska 99708

www.maryshields.com

DEDICATION

To
Alaska

. . . the freshness, the freedom, the farness . . .

Robert Service

CONTENTS

Foreword

PERHAPS IT IS POSSIBLE that one challenging, charming, strenuous, exasperating, real part of Alaska may not disappear altogether after all.

Here is the story of a young woman who, first alone and then in partnership with a stalwart young man, found fulfillment in handling a team of dogs — on the handlebars, on the gee pole, slogging along on snowshoes.

These young people will take you where there are no trails, to parts of Alaska where dogs are still the only possible means of transport. And in the travel they will also give you authentic glimpses of villages and people and ways of life which I hope may yet endure for some time — unfettered ways, harmless, compassionate, and strong. Alaska needs and deserves such ways.

Margaret E. Murie

Introduction

ANY DAY OF THE WEEK you can travel across Alaska for just the cost of a ticket. Climb aboard a shiny airplane, settle back in your plush reclining seat and page through a magazine. You can be whisked from Juneau to Barrow, from Fairbanks to Nome, in a matter of hours.

Halfway through your flight, peer out of that plastic porthole in the sky — the clouds have cleared a bit. The endless peaks of the Alaska Range stretch out as far as you can see. Hundreds of glacial river valleys cut their way through the foothills, beginning their long meander to the sea. One ridge system undulates into the next, and the hills gently roll down to the lowlands.

But look a little harder. Search the crest of that snowy pass. Do you see those tracks in the snow, those thin ribbons unraveling up the valley? Whatever made a trail way out there in the middle of nowhere?

The clouds close in again. Oh well, your imagination was just playing tricks on you anyway.

I've seen those strange tracks myself, and I've followed them far enough to understand their making. The two wooden runners of a dog sled are responsible. If you look closer you'll see many smaller tracks imprinted in the snow between those ribbons. Those are the footprints of Alaskan sled dogs, evidence of the quiet power of the past. Picture yourself down on that trail.

The snow has fallen every day for the past week. It may continue to fall every day of the week to come. Your leg muscles ache with every step each time you lift your showshoe to shake off the accumulation of snow and each time you force your foot forward to gain another two feet.

Shift your weight, shake off the other snowshoe and force that foot forward. Lift after lift, shake after shake, force after force, slowly, slowly you move up the valley, another 10 paces completed; reward yourself with a rest.

A soft command, "O.K.," brings the dogs up behind you a few feet from the tails of your snowshoes. They respect your "winter feet" and they keep a safe distance behind, even though they can't understand why those bits of wood and rawhide are so precious to you. Your dogs don't know that only with those snowshoes can you pass out of this valley of deep snow. Without them you are helpless — floundering, crawling, first sweating and then chilled. In a short time you would be exhausted and long for a short rest in the soft snow around you. From that rest you would never awake.

The narrow sled that drags along behind your team is your home away from home, your security for survival. Those gracefully curved runners and rails, the stanchions mortised in place, strengthened by tightly stretched babiche, flex and give with every undulation of the trail. A sled built with nails or screws would have self-destructed miles ago, but this old friend has proven reliable for many years.

There is comfort in having a piece of home with you, one hundred miles from the nearest cabin in the middle of a February snowstorm in Alaska. The wood of this sled once stood as the straightest-growing birch tree, down by the creek near the home cabin. For 50 years the sapling reached toward the sun and listened to the wind, but swayed only a few feet from where its roots took hold. Fancy that wooden spirit enjoying all this exploring, all this traveling, taking in the sights and sounds of foreign forests. Perhaps at night, long after you are asleep, your vagabond sled creaks tales to the eager seedlings encircling your camp.

Packed securely in your sledload are your tent, Yukon stove, sleeping bag, caribou mat, grub box, cook kit, ax, saw, and two hundred pounds of dog food and tallow. You carry all you need to make a comfortable camp except for firewood and water. All around you are dead trees and gallons of snow. When it's time to stop, your needs will be fulfilled.

How eager the dogs are today. This has been an easy pace for them. They must enjoy seeing you up in front breaking trail for a change. Imagine them barking commands to you," Come on, let's go. Pick it up a little, man. Dig! Dig! Dig!" But they are faithful friends. They have no bitter thoughts. Sometimes their unending faith forces you to live up to their hopes.

Why do they follow you, crossing wild mountains and high rivers? What assures them that you will somehow produce dinner night after night? When you are exhausted and can't go another step you collapse in the snow. Soon a soft muzzle is nuzzling you to your senses. Your inner fire is rekindled and you get up and push on. Do you deserve such unquestioning friendship?

Hey! Wake up! You're daydreaming, consciously extending your rest stop between marches. Time for you to break trail again.

Lift, shake, force, lift, shake, force. There are still a few more hours of daylight left. Maybe you'll gain the pass before dark. Conditions are bound to improve on the other side — maybe windpack, maybe overflow ice, or maybe even windswept tundra. Even if you find more of the same, at least you'll be coasting downhill and that will make a difference.

Your muscles have ached before, but you passed through the slow-going country. You know the next day can bring clear skies and easier trails. You're curious to see the other side of the pass and the long round view from the top. To the north perhaps you'll see the Yukon River and rememeber when you made your way downriver into Rampart.

To the east the Fortymile country rolls out into Canada. One spring these very same dogs carried you into Yukon Territory, chasing gold rush spirits of the Klondike. To the west angles the long Iditarod Trail. Remember the thrill when you first saw the ocean as you coasted down the Kaltag portage into Unalakleet?

Just another mile or two to the top of the pass. This is a good life! Memories of past ramblings make your muscles a little stronger. You forget your aches and cramps. You'll gain the summit yet today, and maybe make camp many miles down the other side. Somewhere above a jet rumbles over. You look up, but the snow clouds keep their secret. Oh well, your imagination was just playing tricks on you anyway.

Chapter 1
I Want to Go Back

I MAY HAVE PICKED IT UP while drinking from a small mountain stream in the Chugach Mountains. I may have inhaled it while breathing the ancient winds blowing in from the glaciers across from Homer. Perhaps I digested it with some blueberries gathered from the tundra near Bethel, or it may have infected my eyes while squinting out at McKinley from Fairbanks. I don't even know when I first became aware of the symptoms, but as I stood there alone in the center of the parade grounds at old Fort Chilkat, waiting for the ferry to begin my journey back to Wisconsin, I knew I had been permanently enchanted by the North.

Speaking to the stars, I recited some lines from Robert Service:

> *It's the great, big, broad land 'way up yonder,*
> *It's the forests where silence has lease;*
> *It's the beauty that thrills me with wonder,*
> *It's the stillness that fills me with peace.*
> *. . . There's a land — oh, it beckons and beckons,*
> *And I want to go back — and I will.*

That summer of 1965 I came to Alaska to work for the Camp Fire Girls as a counselor for their traveling day camp. Free, round-trip transportation made the job irresistible and I accepted with no idea of what I was getting in for.

There under the stars, at the end of that summer, I repeated the last line, *"And I want to go back — and I will."* That was my promise to the stars, and for the next school year those stars reminded me of my oath. Three days after my last exam the next June I departed for Alaska, leaving an explanation for my absence at graduation exercises.

I worked for the Camp Fire Girls again that summer, mostly as waterfront director at the Kenai Lake Camp. At the end of the summer I helped with a day camp near Fairbanks. After the last campfire had smoldered out, the last blackened marshmallow licked off its stick, and the last camper retrieved by her reluctant mother, the equipment was packed up and the old camp truck

1

rumbled off in the dust. The rest of the staff made their way to Fort Chilkat to catch the ferry and return to the Lower 48. To be by myself for the first time was a little lonely, but there wasn't time to sit around and mope. I would winter in Fairbanks, so I had to look for a place to live.

I found a little shed to call home, with rent payable in baby-sitting at the Lawlor home. This amazing 11-member family gave me a warm welcome for my first Alaska winter. Various jobs turned up to pay for my groceries and other needs, and with only the essential material comforts I had space and time to consider some basic questions of life, questions many 21-year-olds were asking themselves in 1966. My answer seemed to be coming from the wilderness.

After two years in Fairbanks I was curious to try living away from the security of the city. My girl friend, Judy MacDonnel, and I found an abandoned cabin along the Alaska Railroad, about halfway between Anchorage and Fairbanks. Judy's plans changed at the last minute, when she was offered a teaching position in the village of Saint Marys on the lower Yukon. I was happy for Judy but a little uncertain about living in the "wilds" by myself. However, my heart was set on the adventure so off I went. This simple decision changed my life.

My winter home waited at the base of the Chulitna Butte, Mile 276½ on the Alaska Railroad. My closest neighbors were 2½ miles down the tracks, and the nearest community was Gold Creek, some 13 miles to the south. Mr. Caudy, one of the neighbors, claimed the abandoned cabin but gave me permission to use it for the winter. It was more than "rustic," and more than "run-down." When I jumped off the train that fine autumn day, my boxes of supplies unloaded into the tall golden grass, I was faced with spending the winter at the "Last Resort."

This location will certainly make up for any deficiencies the cabin might hold, I told myself. From the beaver pond I had a wonderful view of McKinley, and my dream of living near the marvelous mountain was about to come true.

I spent the first two days cleaning up after the previous tenants — squirrels, marten, porcupine and goodness only knows what else. The door was off its hinges, so a little finger banging was in order. I had brought packages of bright blue crepe paper to paper over the dingy old cardboard boxes that insulated the walls. I pinned up the new facade and was delighted with the results. I swept off the cupboard and arranged my supplies.

By the middle of September the nights were already frosty. It was high time to bring in some firewood. I had never heated with wood before, so my first attack on a dead snag was a challenge. Halfway through the cut, my brand-new, red swede saw was pinched and trapped by the lowering log. I came to the saw's

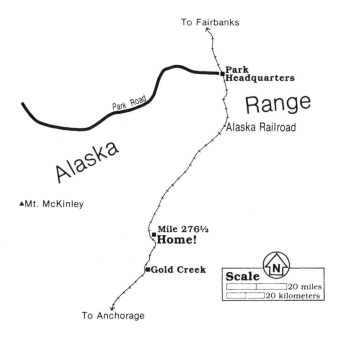

rescue with the double-bitted ax and, after an hour's effort, much cussing and even a few tears, the slightly twisted saw was removed. On top of that, I had an eight-foot, dry log. I dragged the prize home and sawed it up into stove lengths.

The sway of my sawing soon crumbled the old sawhorse, which had weathered along with the cabin, so the next morning I began building a new one. This meant bringing in more wood, but slowly the new creation appeared. The final result brought surprising satisfaction; I was more proud of that little sawhorse than I had ever been of any term paper back in college. It was the first step in what I learned that winter, doing things for yourself. Yes, I made hundreds of mistakes, but they didn't hurt anyone else and I gained experience from each one.

In October my dear friends, Mike and Sally Jones and their young daughter Rebecca, came down from Fairbanks for a visit. For several years the Joneses had lived on the Kobuk River in northwestern Alaska. They were comfortable in my little home, never criticizing my mistakes, but instead gently suggested a few improvements that would make my winter much easier.

I had asked Mike to bring a strong hemp rope from town. On the last day of their visit, we climbed the butte and found the perfect tree for the perfect swing. After the carved seat was notched onto the rope, we each took our turn, swinging to our hearts' content. From that swing, more than one hundred miles of the Alaska Range could be contemplated, with the highest peak in North America, McKinley, only 50 miles to the north. Now my new home was complete.

On the way back from the swing, Sally asked, "Mary, how would you like to borrow our three sled dogs for the winter?"

Mike added, "We have an old freight sled we could send down on the train. The sled needs a little repair, but it should serve you well for hauling water and firewood. We won't be using the team this winter and you might enjoy them."

Back at the cabin, I wrote out a check for my last $80 to cover train fare and dog food. As the northbound train carried the Joneses around the corner, I asked myself, What in heaven's name am I getting in for now? By the time I had walked back to the cabin I had an answer, Maybe heaven!

Three days later the next southbound train squeaked to a stop at the base of the butte. The brakeman, conductor and baggage man checked me out as they handed down the old gray sled. Next, 50-pound bags of dog food were eased down, which I weakly set around my feet. I could see the three excited dogs chained to heating pipes in the baggage car. They were led over to the open door and urged to jump, chains trailing behind them. I managed to catch all three chains. The dogs zoomed around me, terrified by the noise of the engine gearing up. I huddled with my arms around the three frightened creatures until the caboose wobbled by.

At last the quiet returned and I introduced myself to my new companions. A note taped on the sled instructed, "Dear Mary, Good Luck! Kiana is the dark female, Rusty is the fluffy male, and Agean is the younger version of Rusty. Just harness them up and away you'll go! The harnesses are in the bag on the sled. Kiana is the leader. Have fun, Mary! Love, Mike and Sally."

Well, that sounds easy enough, if I can just figure out how to harness up, I said to myself. I tried several styles, finally deciding on one, and tied the dogs to the sled. Away we did not go, at least not all in the same direction. I tried the well-known command, "Mush on, you malamutes!" We didn't mush.

By this time the dogs were hopelessly tangled in their ropes, so I let them loose and dragged the sled back to the cabin myself.

About an hour later, after I had just finished packing in the last 50-pound bag of dog food, the three free spirits returned. I congratulated them on their timing.

One of the bags had suffered a rip during the hauling, and I soon learned that "dog food," not "mush," was the magic word. While the dogs were happily munching away I secured chains to their collars. Suddenly we were a family of four, a nice feeling. I had been enjoying my own company, but these three spirits would be a pleasant addition.

Determined to get at least one dog pulling the sled before sundown, I tried Kiana by herself. This time I coaxed her from in front, and she followed along nicely. I put the water jugs in the sled, "just in case." Down at the creek, I chopped open the water hole and filled the jugs. Twenty gallons of water made a heavy

load for just one dog, but Kiana pulled and I pushed and an hour later we were back with our prize.

Encouraged by this success, I tried Rusty and Agean, and by sunset every vessel capable of holding water was overflowing. That night my dreams took me farther than the creek, and, best of all, Kiana, Rusty and Agean were still there when I woke up.

Over the winter, the country taught me many lessons. Being by myself, I had time to watch and listen. I heard the singing of my own heart, the joys, the fears, the questions, the unanswerables. A peace filled me and gave me strength I had not known before.

By February my supplies were getting low. I left Rusty and Agean with my neighbors while Kiana and I took off for Valdez. I worked in the hospital there for a month, earning enough money to get us through until spring.

Returning to Chulitna in March was exciting and refreshing. Rusty and Agean were happy for our return, and we all resumed our winter life. A few weeks later, Kiana had a semi-surprise for me. I had noticed her belly filling out, but I had ignored it. Despite my strict precautions the Valdez-roving Labrador, normally found sleeping at the gas station, had fallen in love with Kiana. Kiana had fallen into something else, and I had fallen into an instant black dog team, increased overnight by six new pups.

Winter's dark shadows were retreating. As the days grew longer, the temperature hovered above zero and the restless winds swirled hints of sweet-smelling forest around me. The promise of spring was overwhelming.

Flagging down a northbound train, I loaded aboard the old gray sled, my three adult dogs and a cardboard box nesting the six pups. When the train pulled into Mount McKinley National Park (now Denali National Park and Preserve) the entire outfit was unloaded, much to the amazement of the locals who were waiting for their mail to be distributed in the tiny post office that occupied a corner of the station.

The past two summers I had roamed around the park, but this long, cold time was the real test for plants and animals that live there. I wanted to revisit the country in the winter and to know the land under these conditions.

My gear was tied onto the sled and the box of pups was snuggled in back where I could keep an eye on it. When the three adult dogs all were facing in the same direction we took off up the main road. Fortunately there wasn't much traffic in the winter.

The ranger on duty at park headquarters invited me to use the Savage River cabin, if I got that far. I thanked him and continued on my way to the unknown. As I directed the sled up the drifted road, I felt like Admiral Peary. This was the greatest adventure I had ever had.

About seven miles out, the farthest I had dog-sledded in one day, I pulled off the road and made camp. A pair of twin spruce trees offered shallow snow underneath their branches. Kiana was relieved to have her pups with her again and so were the pups, who wiggled in close for a warm meal. They had been sleeping in the box, and had been good passengers. Rusty and Agean were tied to clumps of willows a little way off.

After feeding the dogs, I stretched out in the sled and rummaged through my gear for something to eat. Most everything needed cooking, but I was too exhausted for that. I found some cookies, thawed them out in the warmth of my sleeping bag, had "dinner" and fell asleep.

I was startled awake by a very loud, very close, booming noise. I listened, curled up in my warm cocoon. The booming sounded again, like an extraordinarily great horned owl. I poked my head out to investigate, but immediately recoiled. My first confused impression was that of an enormous yellow eye. I pictured myself in the mummy bag, a tempting, fat blue caterpillar. I waited for the impending clutch of the owl's talons. After a few seconds orienting myself to my new bedroom, I peeked out again. There was the full moon, a golden eye innocently watching the world roll by.

The deep booming echoed again, directly overhead in the spruce. Kiana growled softly and her pups squealed and re-arranged themselves. Then I realized that their squealing was a dinner invitation for the owl. I reached over to soothe a worried mother dog. My movement set the owl's wide wings flapping in retreat. His next threat was muffled in a distant stand of trees.

Marveling at this nocturnal encounter, I lay on my sled wondering why I had wasted the entire winter in the confines of a cabin. The next morning, when I reluctantly crawled out of my warm sleeping bag, I remembered.

My boots were frozen shut, my bare hands were soon stiff, and my throat was begging for a drink. I knew I would warm up as soon as I got moving, so I stuffed my feet into the tight boots, packed the sled, harnessed the dogs and started up the road. After 10 minutes pushing the sled uphill, I was toasty again and my boots were thawed enough to fit more comfortably. We were nearly above tree line, and there on the right side of the road a little spring trickled through the snow. I dug out my camping cup and enjoyed breakfast.

On top of the pass going over into Savage River about an hour later, I anxiously scanned the horizon. To the southwest McKinley sparkled over the tops of the nearby mountains. I was now seeing the Great One from the other side, the north, but I felt comfortable just to be back in the same neighborhood.

From the pass the trail was all downhill into Savage River. I enjoyed three days based at the ranger patrol cabin, cooking real meals on the little stove and faithfully observing the rules posted on the back of the storm door, "Get snow water on the left; pee on the right."

I enjoyed short day trips from the cabin. On the fourth day I climbed the ridge overlooking the Savage River, accompanied by Agean dancing at my feet. On a high point of the ridge I settled down with my binoculars to search for wildlife in the valley below.

I didn't realize Agean had wandered off until I heard his bark from farther up on the ridge. He came bounding back toward me, stopping every few steps to shake his head or paw his nose. The quills protruding from his muzzle signaled the end of my first dog sledding adventure. I returned to the ranger cabin, removed as many quills as I could, then packed the sled and headed back to the train station.

Back home at Chulitna, I continued to remove quills, but Agean was getting extremely tender and his struggling made my attempts useless. My neighbor, Sandy Caudy, came to the rescue. She was an experienced dog de-quiller, and her technique was efficient. First we hogtied Agean and stuffed him into a big U.S.

mail sack (thanks to the Alaska Railroad). Just his head stuck out above the drawstring, and over his eyes we tied a thick bandanna.

I straddled the mound of dog and held his mouth open with a belt looped around his upper jaw. Sandy calmly went in with her needle-nosed pliers, aiming carefully at the broken-off quills. Each surprise attack jerked out a dark, barbed dagger. An hour later, we had cleaned up all the remains we could see, so we let Agean up. He seemed quite relieved and calm. We relaxed, had a cup of coffee, and counted the quills, 27 daggers, which we carefully deposited in the stove.

My last chore of the spring was to find homes for the six black pups. After they were weaned, I bundled them up in their cardboard traveling box, now a bit snug, and we headed off for Talkeetna on the southbound train. My Mile 276 wasn't an official stop, but if I flagged down the engineer he would always halt for me.

Within 24 hours I had found homes for five of the pups. I returned home on the next day's northbound, carrying just one fat black pup curled up in the expanse of his previously crowded box. I called him Cabbage because he was so round and silly looking. His future owner could give him a reasonable name, but Cabbage would do until that time came.

I closed the cabin and returned to Fairbanks to give Rusty, Agean and Kiana back to Mike and Sally. Our parting was a sad one, but I still had Cabbage to keep me company. It was May, and I wanted to go backpacking in McKinley Park before settling down to a summer job.

At the train station I was waiting for my pack to come off the baggage car when a Park Service ranger inquired about Cabbage. I explained that I was looking for a home for the pup.

The ranger's face softened and smiled, "We're looking for some new blood up at the kennels. I think Cabbage would be a nice addition. I'll take him off your hands, if you're sure you want to get rid of him."

I agreed, handed over my little friend, and took off for the tundra. The deed was done, but I immediately missed my dark, furry shadow.

May was a glorious time to explore the back country — no tourists and no mosquitoes. I stretched out my supplies as long as possible, but on the 16th day I returned to the depot to go back to the working world.

The ranger reappeared, pardoned his way through the crowd, and cleared his throat. He politely asked about my wanderings and then got to the point.

"I'm sorry, but I'll have to return Cabbage to you. The other rangers at the kennels insist he has too much Labrador blood in him. The tourists expect our team to look like malamutes, and, well . . . he's a good little dog, I'm sure you won't have any trouble finding him a home in Fairbanks."

So, just when I had almost forgotten about the pup, he returned to my life. I was surprised to see how much he had grown in two and a half weeks. I was even more surprised when he bounded over, responding to his "temporary" name. Perhaps this four-legged, two-eared, one-tailed Cabbage would stay with me after all.

Chapter 2
The Rhythm of the Winter Trail

MY WINTER AT CHULITNA had been a thoughtful time. I had begun to understand myself and what I wanted in life. Although not especially lonely, I regretted not sharing the joys of that simple life with another human being; the alpine glow on McKinley, a walk under the full moon with every twig a-sparkle in the bright night, or just the contentment of a quiet day at the cabin.

The next two years I lived near Fairbanks. I built a little home in a lovely grove of birch trees, in the middle of the Lawlors' homestead. I enrolled at the university, taking biology classes. Various jobs appeared to pay my bills.

In 1970, on a return trip to Chulitna with the Joneses' dogs, Agean disappeared. New snow covered his tracks and my search was in vain. I suspect a moose might have done him in with a well-placed kick. Rusty was ready for retirement, and some dog-loving friends, John Parker and Heidi McIssac, gave him a special home. Kiana returned to her family, the Joneses. Only Cabbage remained with me.

The next winter, Roger Burggraf, a generous neighbor, allowed me to run his dog team several times a week. In March I borrowed a few dogs from Roger, and with Kiana, Cabbage, and some Fairbanks friends, returned to McKinley Park. In just a week's time, our little group doubled my distance of the year before. The trip also doubled my desire for more dog team traveling.

In the winter of 1970 a tall traveler from Wisconsin made his way up the Alaska Highway. To John Manthei's mind Wisconsin's north woods had become too crowded. The special hunting and fishing haunts he had returned to year after year were not the same any more. As he drove along, he hoped Alaska would still have room.

When he reached the crossroad at Tok, Alaska, John read the highway signs: Fairbanks, north 205 miles; Anchorage, south 328 miles. The arctic wind whispered, "Go north, young man," and he followed the wind.

John had said his good-bys in Wauwatosa, only 25 miles from

my home in Waukesha. Although our high schools had been great rivals, we had never crossed paths. Now after thousands of miles our trails were slowly converging. We met at a friend's ice-skating party in November 1971.

We ran into each other again a few weeks later, and decided to go on a sledding picnic, using Roger's dogs. The picnic appealed to John's appetite, big and healthy like the rest of him, and the dog sledding to his spirit. Within the following two weeks he rounded up a dog team of his own, which included Dumb-Dumb, Sad Dog and Gussuk.

Dummy was an experienced lead dog, retired from Dennis Kogl's team in McKinley Park. After 13 years on the trails Dummy was a little deaf and beginning to go blind. John claimed he had a miniature ear trumpet attached to Dummy's collar to help him catch commands, but I never saw it. The old veteran spent most of his time in his doghouse where, John said, he was "typing up his memoirs." We both respected that dog — he had seen 10 times more dog trails than we had.

Sad Dog was a huge, brown sway-backed beast. He was 99 percent heart, with never an unkind thought, except one time when he was innocently curled up asleep in his doghouse and a porcupine waddled down the trail through the dog yard. Dummy and Gussuk leaped to the ends of their chains, snapping and barking at the confused trespasser. The porky scrambled for the nearest dark hole. Unfortunately, that dark hole was the entrance to Sad Dog's house. Awakened from his dreams, the gentle 95-pound beast had no choice but to kill the intruder. When Sad Dog came out he was nearly as prickly as the porcupine had been when he went in. A three o'clock in the morning trip to Dr. Beckley, a Fairbanks veterinarian, saved the dog's life.

Gussuk came from Selawik, an Eskimo village on Kotzebue Sound. Gus had a yellow coat and blue eyes, which explains his name. Gussuk means "white man" in the Ipiutak language (the Kobuk River dialect).

By late winter John was planning a spring trip into the Brooks Range. He needed a smaller sled, so we asked Mike and Sally about borrowing the old gray Chulitna sled. The Joneses generously agreed, and John began repairing it. The smooth lines reappeared; no bandages, no splices, no tape, rope or wire. In the back of the basket, a delicately designed backstop of babiche (rawhide) was laced to represent the four seasons: a sun, a birch leaf, a snowflake, and a dogwood blossom. Several coats of varnish protected the wood from the weather. The contrasting colors of new brown wood and old dark-gray wood were emphasized by this coating. The old sled never looked so proud, sturdy and adventurous.

In March of 1972, John, Dumb-Dumb, Sad Dog, Gussuk and the rejuvenated sled flew north to begin a journey from Wiseman to Anaktuvuk Pass, some three hundred miles round trip. He was gone for six weeks.

Meanwhile friends asked me to join a dog team expedition to Wonder Lake, some 95 miles out in McKinley Park. No winter traveler had ventured beyond the Toklat River since the early dog team patrols of 1940. Visiting the far wilderness under those circumstances would make me feel like an honest explorer, so I accepted without hesitation.

My three companions, Bob Schlentner, John Bryant and Dennis Kogl, were good dog team drivers and I hoped to learn from them by watching how they handled their teams and camped in the cold. My classes could somehow survive a short vacation.

My role was to help where needed. Sometimes I rode the runners of Bob's sled, pulled by the largest team. He would straddle the towline on gee-pole skis (three-foot-long, cut-off downhill skis) guiding the sled from the front and being pushed along as he hung onto the pole. Cabbage was an official member of that team and I was proud of my black friend as he tugged along pulling his fair share.

John Bryant ran only four big freight dogs in his team. When trail conditions were less than perfect (which was most of the way) John would trot along behind his team on snowshoes, keeping the sled on the tracks with the gee pole. Dressed in gray wool union suit and heavy wool pants held up with suspenders, he looked like the traditional sourdough who had spent his life on the trail. The movements of man and dogs, against the background of the snowy mountains, were, in my mind, "The Alaska Ballet."

Dennis Kogl was the trail breaker. He could snowshoe faster than the rest of us could walk. Our steepest climb was going up the east side of Stony Hill. Dennis traversed the slope several times. I stayed with his team, trying to keep the sled from sliding downhill. After several hours of hard climbing we reached the leveling crest. From the top we saw the gentle Thorofare valley, flowing away toward the snowy slopes of McKinley, still some 50 miles away, yet filling the entire view. We stopped for a quick lunch and then glided down the treeless divide toward our goal, Wonder Lake, now only 40 miles away.

By midafternoon, we were out in the middle of a very windy Thorofare River bar. The snow blew around in the air, sparkling and twinkling in the sun. We neared the edge of Muldrow Glacier and, once in the shadow of its canyon, were instantly chilled.

In 1957 the Muldrow surged dramatically, advancing over a mile to create this canyon. Of course the glacier wouldn't budge again for hundreds of years, but my imagination teased with the idea of the ice awaking, leaping forward in one more great push, and squeezing mushers and dogs under the moraine. Tales of mastodons, frozen while munching daisies, were fun to think about, but mushers and dogs? No thank you.

In the very last puffs of twilight we eased out of the canyon and onto a comfortable braided river bar. The warmth of relaxing melted away my glacier fears. A friendly grove of cottonwoods invited us to stay the night. The tents were up in a flash, and the camp stove was pumped up and lit. The men fed their dogs and I fed the men. As they were returning to the big tent for dinner someone yelled, "Look up on the ridge across the river. It's a wolf!"

We all whirled for a glimpse. The wolf trotted along the horizon and disappeared over the other side. We were all quiet for a minute, each absorbing the visit, tucking away the memory for safekeeping.

The next morning I awoke and lit the candle. When I glanced over at John Bryant, still asleep in his big, puffy down bag, I began roaring with laughter. John was covered with a new plumage of white down feathers. They were everywhere, in his hair, in his beard, everywhere. John cracked an eye open to see what was so funny. He too began roaring. I had also sprouted the same white plumage, and my braids were prepared to fly off on their own.

My laughter toned down a bit when I discovered it was my sleeping bag that had provided the decorations. I must have rolled into the warm heating stove during the night before the fire burned out. Our next camp was in the luxurious big timber of the McKinley River bar. We stopped early in the afternoon, lured by the clear open channel which would make feeding dogs and cooking so much easier. We made camp in some nearby spruce trees, and I came back to the channel to fill the Thermoses and pots. The bright pebbles were magnified by the water and their colors were a delight, contrasting with the pure white landscape in front of me.

As I juggled my water containers, I remembered the part in *The Little Prince*, a favorite book from childhood, where the Little Prince is confronted by a merchant selling pills to quench thirst. The pills would save people lots of time, but the Little Prince concluded that, if he had the extra time, he would most like to use it walking toward a spring of fresh water.

As I walked back to camp, I could smell the cottonwood buds that were just beginning to swell with the warmer temperatures. I was very content with my tiny spot in the world. The young winds gave me a new energy, and the old mountains gave me a feeling of peace and understanding. The simple routine of our nomadic life was very satisfying and very appealing. I also wondered about my tall friend, sharing the same spring in the next mountain range to the north, only three hundred miles away.

We reached Wonder Lake the next day. From its cozy location nestled in the Kantishna Hills, the widest view of McKinley could be enjoyed. We remained in the area about a week, taking short day trips to visit friends wintering nearby. A new supply of dog food and people food had been flown into the Kantishna airstrip. We reorganized and finally had to turn around and head back.

Most of our trail was still usable and we covered the miles in half the time they had taken on the way out. All too soon, we were back at headquarters. Our great adventure was over.

Returned to Fairbanks and its melting snow, I promised myself that I would have my own dog team the next winter. John Manthei, out on his first solo trip, was making another promise to himself; he would find a companion to join him on his next cross-country journey. Promises have a way of being kept in Alaska. You don't even have to keep your fingers crossed.

Chapter 3
The Trail Leads On

DURING THE PAST FOUR YEARS I had been apprehensive about accepting the responsibilities of owning my own dog team. Now the time was right to take the big step. Mike and Sally offered Kiana and her two recent pups, Ambler and Kobuk, and this time I could have the dogs for keeps. I also had Luna, the moon dog, a four-month-old pup given to me by a friend, Linda Hewitt. With these recruits and Cabbage, my team was complete.

I bought a birch sled from the Burggrafs for $50. The sled was really a child's size, but the price was right and I loved it. I sanded off the old weathered finish and painted on two new coats of varnish. (Later I learned that spar varnish held up better in the extreme cold.)

Have dog team — will travel, I told myself, but learning the difference between "having" a dog team and "traveling" with one was painful. Innocent, I hooked up all five dogs, slipped the tie-down rope, and set off. We shot out the narrow, winding footpath, ricocheting from birch tree to birch tree.

When we hit the main trail, two options were possible: a 90° turn to the left or a 90° turn to the right. Without any hesitation, we went both ways — and then no ways at all. Kiana, noble lead

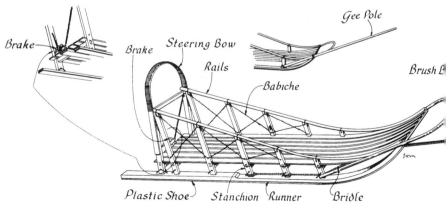

Sled diagram by Willard Manthei

16

dog of the North, stopped to sniff a willow. Before I could get my foot on the brake all five dogs were piled up on top of each other.

There was a low grumble, then a more serious sounding snarl. Before I knew it, all five dogs were growling, curling their upper lips and displaying nasty fangs. The next instant they were on top of each other and the fur was literally flying. I ran forward and pulled dogs off of one another, but they jumped back faster than I pulled them off, tangling everyone, myself included, in the towlines.

Frightening red blotches of blood soaked into the snow and the dogs on the bottom squealed pitifully. I panicked! When my wits returned I tied off the sled and began working from one side. I broke off a sturdy stick and went in swinging. After much screaming, crashing and yelping, I separated the five dogs.

My heart was whacking inside my chest as hard as I had been whacking on the dogs. My arms and legs were shaking, my voice was tense and shrill. I was crying, I was scared, and I was mad!

I fell to the ground glaring at the sorry mess around me. "This isn't the way dog sledding is supposed to be!" I pleaded with the guilty canines, each off by itself, licking its wounds.

I unharnessed the two most suspect culprits and dragged them back to their chains. With the remaining three dogs, I set off again. The tone of my voice meant business and the team tugged along like seasoned champs. This was more like it. I relaxed a bit, but kept my voice serious.

Over the next few weeks I worked with various combinations of dogs and eventually got the five together without an uproar. Dog sledding was as wonderful as I had hoped it would be. Having my own team made a good thing even better.

The team provided refreshing transportation to my job teaching at Willow Ptarmigan School. Peeking out of the classroom window, I could see the dogs curled up in the snow. They were perfectly content waiting for three o'clock to roll around, but I was longing to be on the trail. When the long, yellow school buses

Wheel Dogs   Swing Dogs   Lead Dog

Tow Line   Tug Lines   Neck Lines   PNTC

pulled up and inhaled the children I breathed a sigh of relief. My team and I were on the trail within half an hour.

I lived for the weekends when John and I would go off on our camping trips, each running our own team. Ever since I had met John back at the ice-skating party I had been a little starry-eyed whenever he was around. The more time I shared with him the more I learned to appreciate his company. His honesty, dependability and sense of humor made him special. His considerable size and strength were overshadowed by his gentle consideration of others.

But what I admired most about him was his independent spirit. Even when working at a full-time, high-paying university job, researching the revegetation potential for the trans-Alaska pipeline, John chose to live in a small one-room cabin a mile's walk off the highway. He repaired an old cabin and made a cozy home, and baked his own bread in a wood cookstove. The winter's supply of firewood was neatly split and stacked around the cabin.

Clearly, John had thought things out, set his priorities and then worked hard to live up to them. Compared to my own split-each-day's-wood-a-day-at-a-time philosophy, his organization was impressive. I could see he was down-to-earth, even through the stars in my eyes (which were so temporarily nearsighted, it was remarkable I could even see the moon).

By the middle of winter we were planning a long spring trip. Both of us managed a month's vacation. On the first weekend in March we were traveling south out of Fairbanks on a well-packed snow-go trail cutting through the Tanana Flats. We had looked out at the first hundred miles of the flats from the university campus, now we would experience them close up and see what was on the other side of the mountains.

Co-workers at the Institute of Arctic Biology, where John worked as a research botanist, had told us about the trail. A study of maps gave us a route through the Alaska Range, following a small tributary to its headwaters, climbing over a pass, and then following another small creek down to the Yanert River, a tributary of the Nenana River, which farther downstream flowed into the Tanana.

Even with our 150 pounds apiece, we made good time the first day, but that evening things were a bit unorganized. In the dim light I made a wee mistake when I prepared the main course, a special package of caribou meat to celebrate our first meal on the trail.

I cooked brown rice and added the sizzling caribou meat. At least, that's what I thought I had done. After a few mouthfuls we discovered I had grabbed the hot cereal instead of the rice.

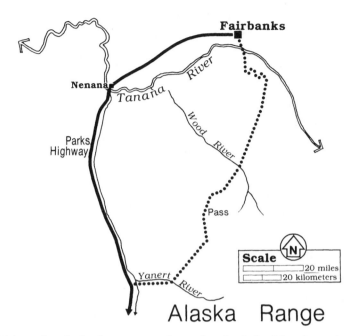

Alaska Range

Although a little disappointed, we finished the bland meal and climbed into our sleeping bags.

The next morning we had just finished breakfast (you guessed it — brown rice) and were on our third cup of coffee when a snowmobile groaned up to the tent. Ron Long, longtime trapper in the area, came in for coffee and wiggled his cold fingers over the stove. He was surprised to find our tracks on the trail and even more surprised to come upon our camp. He kept peeking out at the dogs through the tent flap and explained that he had used a team on his trap line for many years. Now his snowmobile was more efficient. From the look on his face, we guessed he still had a love for the frosty beasts.

He gave us directions for finding the old Busby trail when we reached the end of his packed trail. "It's easy to jog over to the other trail. You can't miss it," Ron assured us as he turned his iron dog toward home and rumbled off. We broke camp, eager to be on our way.

Ron's directions were flawless. We came to the end of his trail in a few miles. Just as he said, there was a little overflow. However, the "easy jog over to the other trail" was not so clear. We followed the ice, but when we hit two inches of wet slush, I was suspicious. I had very little experience with overflow, but John assured me there was nothing to worry about.

"Just relax," he told me. "There's good ice underneath the water. The ice blocks the channel, making the water ooze over the top."

I tried to calm down, but so far as I as concerned, we were up a creek without a canoe, never mind the paddle. At twilight we rounded a corner and found the main channel gurgling along, undercutting a firm snowbank. We camped there and enjoyed the convenient water for cooking. Our disappointment in not finding the trail was soothed by a hot meal. We were exhausted. The spruce-bough bed felt wonderful. We fell asleep hoping the morning would bring better luck.

The sunrise came bright and sparkly, dancing off the hoarfrost feathers that had grown in the night where the moisture from the creek had collected on the twigs and grasses. The water flowed by smoothly. Refreshed and in good spirits, we were confident we would find the trail. After breakfast I started packing up camp while John went off in search of the trail. Just as I stuffed the last sleeping bag, an elated "Yahoo" rang from John's direction. As he returned, the wide smile on his face answered my question.

"Ron Long was right," he said. "It's an easy jog over to the other trail. I don't know how we could have missed it. One thing's for sure, we'll never lose it now."

The dogs sensed our good mood. We folded the tent, packed the sleds, and were on the trail again.

By midafternoon our spirits had drooped a bit. The "old Busby trail" had been great, but it seemed to be going east while we wanted to go south. When we intersected a wide cut, heading due south, we turned eagerly. John had been breaking trail all day, his well-behaved dogs following him.

I tromped as fast as I could, but my team behind me had little patience. They bunched up around me — or on top of me — and always on top of my snowshoes. If they weren't too close, it only meant they were stuck back on the trail. My little sled was not designed to carry a load in its basket. At the slightest curve in the trail the runners would catch in the deep snow and just keep going that way until they were stuck.

Each time it happened I had to make a 180° turnaround on snowshoes. It looked so easy when John did it — just a logical change in direction. He'd pick up one snowshoe and set it down backward, the other leg following smoothly. I got the first half pretty well, but then my other leg never seemed to know where to go. Side-stepping around took much more effort, but eventually I would get myself reversed.

Back to the dogs I'd tromp to free the sled and stand aside. The now well-beaten trail was too fast for me to snowshoe in front of the dogs so I'd follow along, the third time over that same stretch of trail. About the two-hundredth time I returned to the sled, I just sat down in the snow and tried to convince myself this was the only way.

John came back and gave me an arm up. He studied my half-buried sled for a minute and disappeared into the forest. Returning with a young spruce about two inches in diameter, he explained, "What you need is a gee pole. This will help keep your sled on the trail and you on your snowshoes."

He cleaned off the branches and carved the bark from both ends. Lashing the pole to the right or gee side of my sled, John adjusted the handle end to a comfortable height for my right hand. I stood in front of the sled, straddling the towline. A three-foot extension was added to the towline, providing a little more room. The sled looked ridiculous with the pole sticking forward almost the length of the sled itself. I felt even more ridiculous as I prepared to see just how fast I could really snowshoe.

The dogs surged ahead. I paddled along for all I was worth, clinging to the gee pole. In my excitement, I resorted to far stronger superlatives than the appropriate "Gee!" After the team settled down, I managed to stay ahead pretty well and the sled steered with ease.

About a mile farther, the cut we were following dead-ended in a big circle. We sat on John's sled and pulled out the coffee. The steam frosted John's glasses, but thawed our disappointment. With a suspicious tone in my voice I asked, "Aren't we somewhere near the air force bombing range?"

"No," John answered, shaking his head and thawing his glasses with his warm breath, "we're smack-dab on top of it."

We turned the teams around and backtracked the hard-won mile. Again it was time to camp, and again we were not even on the right trail. We strung up the tent across the clearing and chained out the dogs. There had been no tracks on the trail all winter, so it seemed a safe place to camp.

After dinner, John mended a spark hole in the tent while I snowshoed out to look for the trail. The moon was nearly full. Hope was renewed when I found some old blazes that seemed to be going south, more or less (probably less, but anything was better than a dead-end bombing range).

When I returned to the tent about 45 minutes later, John had a spooky look on his face and an equally spooky story to tell.

"You're not going to believe this, Mary, but so help me it's the truth. I was mending the spark hole when I heard this clankety-clank off in the distance. I kept listening and the noise got closer. I know this sounds impossible, but it sounded like a tank. It was coming right toward our camp. In 10 minutes, the sound was so close I went out to try to stop it before it ran over the dogs and the tent.

"I couldn't see it. The sound seemed to be coming through the brush, not down the trail. Then it stopped. I heard two guys get out, clank around on the metal, and swear at something that had broken. Then, so help me, the noise clankety-clanked back where it had come from. Didn't you hear it?"

"No, John, all I heard was a boreal owl hooting. Are you sure you haven't been nipping at the alcohol? I guess when you camp in the middle of a bombing range you must put up with a few ghost tanks in the night."

"You mean things that go clank in the dark?" John added.

After hot cocoa spiked with a little nip, we formulated our First Law of Dog Sledding: Never — never — ever camp in the middle of the trail.

The next day we made better time. The trail I had found proved worthwhile. We spent most of the day on snowshoes, but we were aiming in the right direction. About the middle of the afternoon my dogs gave a little tug. I looked up to see John taking off his snowshoes. A few steps later I understood why; we had come upon a packed trail.

The dogs were as happy as I. They zoomed off to catch the other team. I went for a little ride, sitting on the brush bow, snowshoes dangling in front of me. I hung onto the gee pole as if my life depended on it. (It did!) When we reached John I climbed out and lashed my webs on top of my load. Back on the runners, where I belonged, I relaxed and enjoyed the ride. In the next two hours we tripled our mileage for the day.

Just before sunset the trail opened onto the north bank of Wood River. The wide, braided stream spread out with bank-to-bank glare ice, blue and green in the low sunlight. The idea of going out on that ice the next morning was disconcerting. I concentrated on making camp in a grove of cottonwoods. Just when we had finished the outside chores and were ready to move into the tent, the sun melted its way down onto the western edge of the ice, warming the glacier with an iridescent rosy glow. The enchantment lasted only a few minutes, but the spell quieted us for several hours.

After a gooey pot of macaroni and cheese, we blew out the last candle and nestled into our warm sleeping bags. The fire was soon out; the cold moved in. We guessed the temperature to be about 30° to 40° below zero. The river ice moaned and boomed, popped and snapped. Moonlight decorated the tent with cottonwood shadows. I wanted to stay awake to listen and watch, but the nip on my nose forced me to snuggle down in my sleeping bag, bringing in my wool sweater for company.

I awoke to find the tent already bright with the first cold light of dawn. Delicate frost feathers, our night's breath captured in ice, dangled from the seams in the tent and from the colorful assortment of socks, mittens and boot liners hanging on the ridge rope. The slightest bump to the tent would send down a blizzard of crystals. We tried to shake them down systematically, but they stuck to their own cruel tactic of seeking out warm skin and melting there. After we swept away the accumulated drifts, I lit the kindling. The irresistible reveille of crackling fire, bacon sputtering in the frying pan, and the coffee boiling in the tall can seemed to be the best possible way to start the day.

The river ice was back to its normal blue-green magnificence. I felt rested and eager. Apprehensions of the night before were gone. Camp was folded and divided into the two sleds. The dogs were harnessed and the stake-out chains packed in the sled bags.

I let the tie-down rope slip free. The dogs shot ahead, aiming straight for the high bulge in the ice. The sled swung around as though it were the end skater in crack-the-whip. I prepared for the plunge into the water I knew waited on the other side.

When I opened my eyes again I was delighted to see more ice in front of me. The dogs tore along as if they enjoyed it. And why not? On the ice the sled gave little resistance and the dogs were almost running free. The slight tension on the tug lines seemed to help steady the creatures. Toenails tap-danced along — we were flying.

"I think I'm going to like this river travel," I murmured to the dogs. They just pranced on as though they had been running on ice all their lives.

Soon we were 20 miles upriver. Indeed the ice was nothing to fear. It was an open road going our direction.

Two days later we pulled into Lynn and Sammy Castle's hunting camp. The dogs were staked out in the willows behind the cabins and the sleds were lashed close by. I was a little worried that the free-grazing packhorses might get into the sleds or harm the dogs, but John teased away my concerns.

The next morning when we visited the dogs we found my sled tarp nibbled to shreds in several places. Fortunately all the food was in John's sled, wrapped in an undisturbed canvas tarp. Nothing inside my tarp was touched either, just the tarp itself. Were those horses trying to eat the red and yellow flowers that bloomed on its bright green background?

After a pleasant visit with the Castles we continued on our way. Again we were on snowshoes, climbing a little creek valley that led over a mountain pass to the Yanert River valley. Once we were above tree line the wind broke trail for us. The wind broke almost everything up there. Lynn Castle had invited us to use his shelter, a small plywood building near the top of the pass, but we found it blown over on its side. We tipped it back up and looked inside.

"What a mess!" John shouted out the door. "Everything's upside down in here, but at least there's no wind. Let's start cleaning up."

The next morning we continued side-hilling our way to the crest of the pass. To help keep the sleds from dragging the dogs downhill, we looped the bridle through the downhill runner and then reattached it to the towline. This angled the front of the sled uphill and solved the problem.

The easy joy ride down the other side of the pass, over long stretches of wind-packed snow, was delightful. Down in the creek bed the overflow ice bubbled up in cool blues and greens. We made good time to below tree line where the snow was deep again — back to snowshoes. After two days tromping along the winding course of the creek we reached the wide, glacial-fed Yanert River. We were surprised to find a fair amount of water flowing over the ice.

A few miles downstream it became an unfair amount. The main channel was open. There was no time to consider options and all we could do was "keep on dogging." The dogs splashed ahead on command, but they looked worried.

Three days later we were safely back on a dry, snowy trail turning into Deneki Lakes, a small settlement of a half-dozen cabins near the Parks Highway. With Dennis Kogl and other friends, we made short trips off the Denali Highway, beyond Cantwell. Dennis was driving to Fairbanks in a few days and offered us (all 13) a ride. Our job responsibilities were waiting, so we packed up and returned home.

Our narrow path through the Alaska Range had drifted over almost as quickly as we passed, but in our hearts and dreams the trail was clearly there, leading to many winter journeys to come.

Chapter 4
Long Trails for Short Days

BEING A WAITRESS in Fairbanks brought in good money, not to mention the yummy food scraps taken home for the dogs. When I served lasagna and veal parmesan at Gambardello's the dogs barked in Italian. When it was wiener schnitzel and sauerbraten at the Switzerland their howling took on a distinctive yodel.

I worked as a waitress in the summer so I could run dogs in the winter. When the money ran out in the winter I returned to being a waitress at night so I could run dogs during the day. Those dogs were dictating my life!

Perhaps I was getting a little carried away, but I was too eager to wait for spring. Why not celebrate Christmas and New Year's with a winter trip? We would visit Bob and Carol James, trapping near Manley Hot Springs, and the Hardy family at Tanana.

On December 23, 1973, I mushed out to John's state land selection to pick up the wall tent. We had built a cache there the previous spring, and the tent was home when we visited. I packed up the tent and met John and Stan Parkerson the next day on top of Murphy Dome, about 30 miles northwest of Fairbanks. Stan was on Christmas vacation from high school, and would travel on skis.

We hoped to find the old telegraph line running from Dunbar on the Alaska Railroad to Manley Hot Springs on the Tanana River. We found the abandoned trail, but the regrowth of willows and alders that flourished along it made the going slow. When crossing the many swamps and lakes of Minto Flats we could usually depend on a compass reading, follow it faithfully across the opening, and then hunt around back in the forest until we found the trail again.

On Christmas Eve we pitched tent between the deep banks of Little Goldstream Creek. The 10-foot-wide creek bottom was the only open spot in the thick underbrush. Cold stars twinkled festively. I decided on the "Star of Bethleham" and caroled to John and Stan from outside the tent. My Christmas wish had been answered: we were on the trail.

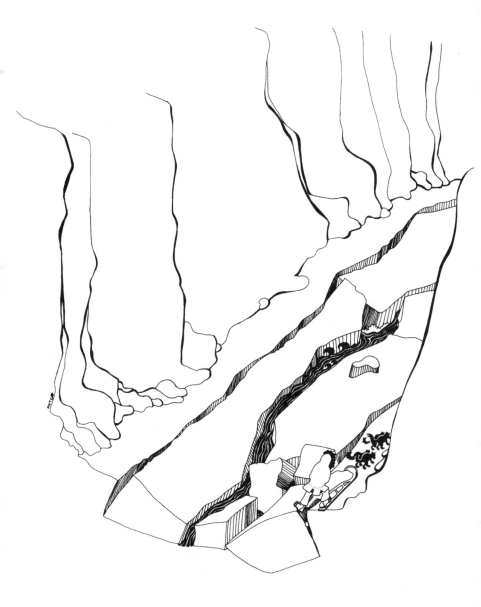

We reached Old Minto, a once active Indian village on a sunny curve of the Tanana River. After the 1967 flood the people moved their village to the north edge of Minto Flats. Most of the old, weathered log cabins looked to be in good shape. A boardwalk connected the main clusters of cabins. I pictured how it had been, smoke curling up from the stovepipes and snow machines parked in front of the cabins. The dog yards would be behind in the willows. Unfortunately some of the buildings had been vandalized; windows had been broken and crude slogans spray-painted on the walls.

The snow was fairly deep that year and trail breaking was an effort. John and Stan took turns up in front while I handled the sleds, freeing them when they got off the track or wedged behind a willow. The telegraph wire was still draped in the trees or from tripods, which helped us find the trail where the willows had moved in.

After a few days at this creeping pace we intersected a packed snow-go trail at right angles to our path. Tempted by the chance to ride for a change, we eagerly bounded off to the east. Stan grasped the tie-down rope and zipped along behind the sled on his skis. After several miles of this fun, when we stopped for a coffee break, John suggested that perhaps the trail wasn't really getting us any closer to Manley.

Stan and I outvoted him. Off we dashed again. Where else could it be going? I asked myself. Of course it will swing around to the north and we'll be in Manley in no time.

But the trail didn't swing around to the north. After another four miles it swung around in a 10-foot loop and headed back on itself — a dead end. Impossible! I told myself. Had we gone seven miles out of our way, only to backtrack another seven miles? We had indeed.

We made camp that night at the spot where our snowshoe tracks ended at noon. The next day we resigned ourselves to breaking trail again. After two miles we came on another fresh trail. This time the track went down the center of a huge cleared transect. Surely this was going to Manley. Stan and I again outvoted logical John.

After four more miles in the wrong direction we admitted our mistake and returned to the deep, unbroken trail. (Stan and I avoided John's I-told-you-so look.) That night after dinner we promised to obey our newly proclaimed Second Law of Dog Sledding: Don't be tempted by broken trails that go in the wrong direction.

These midwinter days were short for traveling. We woke up in the dark around seven o'clock, and were on the trail by dawn, about half past eight. Some nights we continued in the moonlight, but usually we made camp at dusk, about half past three, or four o'clock. That gave us a good three hours in the tent, to read or talk as dinner was prepared. Our insufficient candle supply was rationed to stretch all the way to Manley where we hoped to buy more.

We celebrated New Year's Eve by cooking dinner over an open fire, enjoying the bright full moon. Because the trip was taking longer than we had planned, our food supply was running low. Dinner that night was a white wonder — instant mashed potatoes, popcorn, vanilla pudding and alcohol. The menu might not win the approval of nutritionists, but it did fill us up.

We stood around the campfire, drying our wet pants legs. On the first night of the trip Stan had burned a hole in his new down parka. John lectured him on the need to be more careful on the trip, where an individual's equipment was crucial for everyone's safety.

As we stood with our backs to the fire, John smelled something burning. He warned Stan, who had his hands clasped behind him, but his cuffs passed inspection. A few minutes later the stink of singeing fabric prompted John to repeat his advice. Stan stepped into the deep snow and packed his cuffs, but the stink continued. Stan gleefully pointed to the glowing circumference of a two-inch hole in the back of John's whipcord pants. As John sat in the deep snow, we all roared with laughter.

We pulled into Manley on New Year's Day, at 30° below zero. After making camp we headed directly for the hot springs bathhouse. Chuck Dart, accurately described as "an island of sanity," gave us fresh towels and showed us the trail to the steaming warmth.

The flashlight beam sparkled in the frosty interior of the small plywood building. At one end were benches to hold your clothing; at the other end was a stepped pool with water rushing in at one corner. To lower your freezing body into the water felt unbelievably wonderful. The swirling water melted away tension and sore muscles. Submerging completely was a little scary, mostly because of the dark. If I stayed under for very long, I felt woozy from the heat. To be clean, warm, and relaxed was a refreshing way to start the new year.

We returned the towels to the Darts' house and caught a whiff of something wonderful floating from the kitchen. Chuck casually asked if we had time to stay for dinner. We knew we couldn't get our supplies from the post office until the next day, and all accepted at the same instant. When the pork roast, baked potatoes, sweet potatoes, salad and rolls were set on the table, we tried politely, patiently to pass the platters around, taking appropriate portions. We flat-out devoured everything Mrs. Dart set on the table. When we apologized, explaining our embarrassing appetites, she brought out seconds and even some thirds. We certainly abused their generous hospitality, but we most sincerely appreciated it.

After all the last cake crumbs and tea were finished, we helped clear the table. On the sink, John spied the roaster pan, holding about an inch and a half of solidified grease and some tidbits of pork. Gladys offered the fat for our dogs, but John's disappointed expression won him the prize. At six feet, six inches and two hundred pounds, John describes himself as a "hungry string bean." We watched in amazement as he cleaned the roaster, a satisfied smile on his face.

The next day we picked up our supplies, bought some candles at the general store, and headed down the Tanana River for 50 miles to visit some friends who were trapping in the area for the winter. Stan had arranged to be picked up by a small plane at a nearby airstrip; his school was back in session. We had enjoyed his company and his help breaking trail. He had survived the hungry times with a sense of humor. We missed his much-repeated punch line, "Don't I smell something burning?" during the rest of our trip.

After an enjoyable three-day visit with our friends, including an eating extravaganza featuring whole moose ribs barbecued over a campfire, we continued on our way to Tanana.

Just a few miles outside the village, where the Tanana flows into the Yukon River, was an awesome, old abandoned Episcopal mission built in 1896. Broken windows betrayed the smooth arched lines of weathered timbers, but there was an overwhelming serenity in the sanctuary's setting, high on the bluff overlooking the meeting of the two great rivers. Quiet graves rested in the peace of their picket fences in the front yard.

In Tanana we stayed with the Hardy family, friends of John. Bob Hardy was a public health doctor at the hospital. This family treated us royally. Bob knew of some dogs for sale, so he directed us to Roy Folger's cabin. Roy walked us through his dog lot, giving us a little background on his line of dogs. He spoke honestly and we trusted his opinions.

The two dogs for sale were Morgan and Ole, who were past their prime for race dogs. Roy suggested we take them for a test run and we returned with a little team and a sled. Morgan, a one-time "20-mile-an-hour lead dog," took advantage of his home turf and zipped us around corners and down back trails. Ole pulled steadily and fitted in perfectly.

We were sold — and so were Morgan and Ole. We paid $100 for the pair and took the dogs back to our stake-out chain. That night at feeding time, some villagers came by to look at our dogs. When they recognized Morgan, they commented, with a suspicious smile, "Oh, you've got Morgan now!" Old 20-mile-an-hour Morgan had made the rounds of many Tanana teams. We weren't quite sure that was a good sign, but we were pleased with him.

We headed back toward Fairbanks the second week in January, taking the overland Fish Lake trail rather than the river. Tanana was officially a dry village, but a well-beaten trail to Manley's liquor store was kept open all winter. We averaged 40 miles per day on the good trail, quite a contrast to our earlier 5- to 6-mile average. Between Manley and Dunbar, we passed two of our December's camps in an easy day's travel. As I rode along on the runners, remembering the slow snowshoeing, I felt quite smug.

My bold confidence teased my spirit to daydream . . . if we made it to Tanana in the middle of winter, why not make it to Nome in the spring? I had faith in my dogs. They weren't fast, but they were strong and steady. Before I turned onto the home trail my decision was made — I would try the 1974 Iditarod Trail Sled Dog Race.

Chapter 5
You've Come a Long Way, Baby!

SUDDENLY March 1, 1974, was a reality. My entry fee was paid, my half-ton of supplies was waiting at the checkpoints. In three more days I would be mushing down the Iditarod Trail. My dogs were in good shape. If anything, they were a bit sour after the two thousand miles they had run already that winter. The three-day rest in Anchorage, waiting for the start, would be good for their spirits.

I had confidence in my original six dogs. In the miles together that winter they had won my respect. I also had picked up two new dogs, to put me one over the required seven-dog minimum starting team. They came highly recommended but, after only a month's time with them, I was not too sure of their capabilities.

The Iditarod mushers' meeting was held in an Anchorage hotel on March 2. Making my way through the smoky lobby, bustling with reporters and race fans, I sensed an unexpected flurry of doubt drifting around in my stomach. As the meeting got down to business, I realized I was indeed in a RACE. The other mushers were quite serious about the competition, and especially the prize money. Some peppery discussions about certain race rules revealed lively personalities. The longer the meeting dragged on the more those flurries whirled around in my stomach.

Wilbur Sampson, a racer from Noorvik, beamed at me from across the long table. He had his "Hello, my name is . . ." sticker stuck to his forehead, upside down. Relieved to find a sense of humor in the tense room, I beamed back.

At last the meeting adjourned and the mob pushed upstairs for the banquet. I asked if someone else would draw my starting number and, with great relief, escaped, seeking John and some Fairbanks friends. We walked outside, into the cool, dark, refreshing air. I tucked my arm under John's elbow. A few tears that seeped out of my eyes must have been those stomach flurries melting, because I felt a whole lot better after we walked a few blocks. We stopped at a brightly lit, greasy little cafe and crowded into a booth, sharing fries and hamburgers.

March 4, 7:30 A.M. My dogs and sled were unloaded at Tudor

The Iditarod Race

The first race, conceived and organized by Joe Redington, Sr., of Knik, began in Anchorage on March 3, 1973, and ended April 3, 1973, in Nome. Of the 34 who started the race, 22 finished. The Iditarod has been run every year since its inception in 1973. In 1976 it was declared Alaska's official sled dog race by Gov. Jay Hammond. That year also, Congress designated the Iditarod as a National Historic Trail.

Following the old dog team mail route from Knik to Nome blazed in 1910, the trail crosses two mountain ranges, follows the Yukon River for about 150 miles, runs through several bush villages, and crosses the pack ice of Norton Sound.

Strictly a winter trail because the ground is mostly spongy muskeg swamps, the route attracted national attention in 1925 when sled dog mushers, including the famous Leonhard Seppala, relayed three hundred thousand units of life-saving diphtheria serum to epidemic-threatened Nome. However, as the airplane and snowmobile replaced the sled dog team, the trail fell into disuse. Thanks to Redington, the trail has been assured a place in Alaska history.

Each year the Iditarod takes a slightly different course, following an alternate southern route in odd years (see map). While the route is traditionally described as 1,049 miles long (a figure that was selected because Alaska is the 49th state), actual distance is close to 1,200 miles.

Today, up to 50 mushers from all over the world come to Anchorage in March to run the world's longest — and richest — sled dog race. The Iditarod purse ($100,000 in 1982) is divided among the first 20 finishers. And the race can be close: In 1982, second-place finisher Susan Butcher was only 3 minutes and 43 seconds behind winner Rick Swenson.

From The ALASKA ALMANAC®

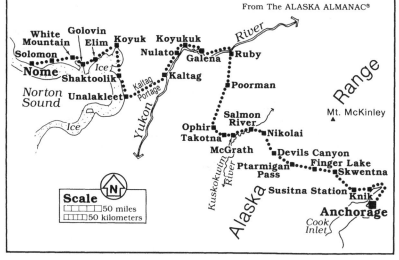

Race Track. A race official checked my required survival gear: a saw, sleeping bag, snowshoes, and emergency rations for myself and the dogs. A bundle of special Iditarod envelopes was added. These were a moneymaking venture for the race committee and would be sold in Nome after they had been sledded over the trail.

John and I walked around admiring other teams and sleds and recognizing famous mushers. Seeing how others solved the same problems we had tackled was most interesting; tarps, techniques of packing loads, sled bags and stake-out arrangements — each musher had something to offer.

Promptly at 9:00 A.M. the race began. The number one starting position was reserved in honor of Leonhard Seppala, representing the team of original Iditarod mushers who relayed the diphtheria serum from Nenana to Nome in 1925. A moment of respectful silence followed the call for him, in remembrance of the heroic efforts of mushers and dogs who had rescued Nome from the feared epidemic.

After the hush, the pandemonium of eager race teams lunging at the invisible starting line permeated the air. Cabbage and Company, tethered on their stake-out chain, watched the first teams take off, never dreaming where the day's trail would lead them.

Team after team of yipping, leaping huskies roared down the starting chute, around the oval track, and out the exit at the far corner of the field. Again and again the announcer boomed, "4-3-2-1 and they're off," and another team sprinted out of sight, loping away as wild as any fresh team at the North American Dog Sled Championships, a speed race.

These are long-distance dogs setting off for a thousand-mile jaunt? I asked myself, very much impressed. As I harnessed my team, I looked with second thoughts at my eight calm dogs, the smallest team in the race, and possibly the least enthusiastic. I knew they would never lope all the way around the track, and my real fear was that Cabbage would play one of his favorite tricks right there in front of everyone.

Cabbage understands that the shortest distance between two points is a straight line. On many previous occasions, Cabbage has taken shortcuts, diagonally across an arc, rather than follow the longer trail around. Cab casually watched all 37 teams take off in front of him, faithfully following the set track. I hoped he was not planning a creative breakthrough at the last moment. The swarm of butterflies beating around in my stomach was lifting me off the ground.

Again the loudspeaker began its countdown, "4-3-2-1," and we were off! John rode on top of my load, not to hold back the team, as other handlers had, but to help me drag Cabbage back onto the track if he tried his shortcut.

After the first thousand yards of galloping my team settled into the natural trot they had been trotting all winter. The announcer joked with the crowd, "Well, there's a team that knows they've got a long trip ahead of them."

An embarrassed laugh rose from the bleachers and a little cheer of encouragement. In seconds we were at the exit and John jumped off the sled, giving me a quick good-by kiss. The butterflies metamorphosed into tears again and slipped down my cheeks. My last look at John, the crowd and the race track was blurred.

Within the next hour the remaining five teams to start behind me all had passed smoothly. They disappeared down the flat trail ahead as though they were rolling down a steep hill. But the butterflies and tears were gone, all fluttered away, all dry and clear. On the runners of my dear little sled, with my good friends pulling me along, I was on my way out of the big city. No more teams left to sneak up on me. I relaxed and enjoyed the scenery, smiled a little, and let loose with a cheery rendition of "These Are a Few of My Favorite Things." The dogs perked up, waved their tails, and looked back over their shoulders. All was back to normal.

A road crossing appeared. We managed it smoothly and disappeared into the woods again. Next, the trail paralleled a long fence plastered with spectators. No one said much as we passed by only 10 feet away, but at the end of the fence a man shouted, "You better turn back now, while you're still close to civilization. You'll never make it to Nome!"

Those words sank deep and hurt. I had never once doubted that we would make it. I told myself, maybe he's really concerned for my safety. I considered his warning as we glided down the trail, Cabbage striking out a nice pace, his tail forever wagging like a metronome.

I called softly to Luna, "Do you want to run all the way to Nome, old girl?" Wag, wag, wag. "Hey Ole, how about seeing the Yukon again?" Wag, wag, wag. I thought again of the man's warning. "Maybe that poor devil never has stood on the back of a dog sled," I said out loud. "We'll never make it to Nome? You just watch us, buddy! Come on Cabbage, let's fly on to the ocean! Yaaa-hooooo!"

As the sunlight faded my spirits brightened. I was still in last place, but we were clipping along nicely. My dogs loved to travel in the dark. Suddenly they burst ahead with a surge of energy. In the shadows ahead I could see something — a moose, a dog team?

The blur focused into a dog team. My chasers caught up in no time and the musher pulled over to let me pass. Now the dogs were really excited and they kept zooming along. Another team appeared and I didn't have to say a word. We steadily gained and caught up. The mushers let me pass. Several times when my voice was heard there were gasps and curses aimed at dogs. To be passed by a woman was quite a blow to some male egos. I felt bad that their dogs suffered.

The first checkpoint was at Knik Lake, some 60 miles from Anchorage. In the dark I could only guess at the country around me. To my left I sensed the ocean or tide flats, with the trail clinging along the edge of an old forest. The wind came in from the water, creaking and moaning in the trees. About one in the morning I reached Knik and was surprised to learn that I placed 26th. Having started 36th, this was quite encouraging.

I spent the night at Knik and awoke to a clear sky, with the wind still howling. The dogs were drifted over where they slept. After rousing them, I was relieved to see everyone stand up, shake off, and appear quite normal. Most of the teams had taken off, some before daybreak.

The trail was in perfect condition, except for steep hills where more than 30 sled brakes had dug a furrow down the middle of the trail. Even standing with both feet on my brake, I could barely touch bottom. Throughout the day I passed or was passed by several teams. My roaring along of the night before was over. The team settled into their normal traveling trot.

We were on the Iditarod Trail, the historic route for traveling to the gold rush towns along the way to Nome. How many thousands had traveled before me, dreaming of rich strikes and gold to last a lifetime? How many had returned down the same trail the following season, disappointed, in debt and discouraged? How many had stayed in the country, finding their fortune either in gold or simply in the search? I remembered Robert Service:

> There's gold, and it's haunting and haunting;
>   It's luring me on as of old;
> Yet it isn't the gold that I'm wanting
>   So much as just finding the gold.
> It's the great, big, broad land 'way up yonder,
>   It's the forest where silence has lease;
> It's the beauty that thrills me with wonder,
>   It's the stillness that fills me with peace.

Again the words held special meaning for me. I fancied I would have stayed along the trail, maybe setting up a roadhouse or, better yet, getting a mail contract and mushing the mail over my section of the trail. So I daydreamed as we made our way on to Skwentna, on to Finger Lake, on to Ptarmigan Pass.

The howling wind increased to a roar and I was thankful for my long kuspuk, a traditional Eskimo woman's parka that ruffled out around my knees. Long wool underwear topped with a thick wool sweater and blue jeans kept me warm inside the corduroy kuspuk. Gail Mayo, my neighbor in Fairbanks, had made me a pair of lightweight wind pants. These were huge and could be slipped easily over boots. The cuffs had yards of drawstrings. When I laced them over the tops of my boots, they made a tight seal. If necessary, I could step into deep overflow and the water would freeze on the wind pants before it seeped into my socks. This feature was a foot saver many times.

Starting to climb Ptarmigan Pass, our route through the Alaska Range, I traveled with Red Fox Olson, a fellow musher from Fairbanks. We saw a team ahead of us, dogs curled up on the snow, the musher sitting in his sled, a glazed expression on his face.

"How long have you been sitting here?" asked Red.

"I don't know . . . a long time . . . a long time. Dogs can't make it up that pitch — too steep. I'm too cold to go farther . . . can't go any farther . . . too cold . . . no farther . . ." the musher repeated.

Red and I exchanged looks and decided to make camp. The dejected musher had a large tent on his sled so we turned around and went down in the lee of the ridge we had been climbing. Along the creek a few willows stuck up above the snow. We struggled with the big tent, losing the battle to the wind several times. After an hour or more, we finally had it stretched up and secured between the three sleds.

Snowshoes were dug in to hold the ends of the stake-out chains — not ideal, but we didn't have much choice. Inside the dark canvas tent, Red's camp stove was pumped up and we all enjoyed a cup of hot coffee. Lolly Medley, the other woman racer, pulled in a few hours later and joined us for the night.

A little warm food, a hot drink and some human companionship revived the quiet musher. He seemed to be doing a lot of thinking, but his spirits improved.

The wind wailed all night and the tent bellowed, flapped, and surged but remained upright. With the first sunlight we were ready to get moving. The first view out the tent flap was frightening; not a nose, ear or tip of a tail could be seen where the night before four dog teams had been standing. I went over to where my team should have been and found eight little steam geysers vented up through small blowholes in the wind-packed snow. I dug with a panicked heart, and just below the surface there was a cozy, black Cabbage, snug in his nest but happy to see me. The excellent insulation of the snow had protected him throughout the night. I moved along the row of blowholes. All the dogs were alive. When unburied they stretched and tried to shake out the packed snow that had plastered their windward sides.

Breaking camp broke all speed records. We knew we would warm up as we climbed the steep pitch that was waiting for us. Lolly, Red and I took off and gained the ridge without too much trouble. The fourth team made a half-hearted attempt and then gave up, probably repeating their performance of the day before. The dogs were overfed malamutes, strong, yet lacking desire. Red Olson took out his long bull whip, went back and masterfully cracked it over their heads. They woke up with astonishing energy and scrambled up the pitch in front of them, dragging their even more astonished master behind them. Red and I shared a good laugh.

The wind was steadily picking up, scouring the high tundra pass bare in many places. Tussocks of dry grass were exposed as far as we could see. All traces of the trail were a hundred miles downwind by then, but the lay of the land showed the probable route. We were gathered together in front of my team, planning our strategy, when suddenly our dogs began to bark.

Four teams appeared on the crest of the pass and swept toward us, carried by the wind. They were a magnificent sight, screaming over the half-bare, half-snowy tundra, looking for all the world like Arabs racing over the desert on long-tailed stallions. When the two caravans met we learned of their night's vulnerable camp and their urgency to retreat below the tree line. We respected their story, for our own night's camp had been windy enough, and it had been sheltered in the lee of the ridge.

The eight teams returned down the trail to a hunting camp a few miles back. During the 1973 race some mushers had abused the privilege of using the camp; this year the welcome mat was not out. The winter caretaker had strict orders not to allow mushers to move in, but, considering the severe weather, he was pressured into radioing Anchorage to see if the owners would relent. Weather reports estimated the winds coming over the mountains to be gusting to 40 miles per hour, giving a wind chill temperature of -110°. Eventually about a dozen mushers accumulated at the camp and were allowed to wait out the storm.

Even though I had my wall tent and stove, I also stayed at the camp, enjoying the chance to get to know some of the mushers. I was surprised that so many of them were without extra food for themselves and their dogs. Sacrificing safety for speed when crossing a high mountain pass seemed foolish to me. When they radioed out, demanding that the race committee fly in emergency supplies, I was disgusted. If they were willing to risk traveling light for the sake of racing then they should live with the consequences, although I hated to see the dogs go hungry. When the wind let up a bit the second day, I was anxious to hit the trail.

On top of the pass the wind was still roaring. My cheeks and wrists were frostbitten from the day before. The new nipping was painful, but I was better prepared this time. Tony Baluta, a racer from Nondalton on Lake Iliamna, showed me a clever idea to protect my wrists. We cut off a pair of wool socks at the heel. A strip of wool was stitched to either side, making a thumb strap when the cuff was slipped over my wrist. This extra layer of wool sealed the exposed skin between my mitten and my parka cuff. For my cheeks, I just pulled my wool scarf up as best I could.

Tony and I traveled the pass together, guessing where the trail had been. Once over the crest we dropped down into a deep, drifted creek bottom running off the pass to form the headwaters of the Kuskokwim River. The deep snow was slow going. Underneath the snow were long stretches of wet overflow. Cabbage, true to his Labrador background, led us through the deep places and eventually we got back onto the wind pack. From the middle of the valley we could see a high and dry route above us and we guessed the trail had probably been up there.

Tony took the lead entering Devils Canyon. The temperature was cold as hell, but the glare ice made traveling so easy we were lured to keep going after dark. For the first time my heavy sledload offered no extra drag and the dogs picked up their pace by a mile or two an hour. I thought about the devil and his canyon. Only in the North have I heard people say "cold as hell." Did it come from the painful burning sensation when a frozen foot or hand thawed out?

The sound of rushing water jerked me out of my fantasy. The devil had tempted us into a dangerous situation. We headed for high ground and made camp.

Tony showed me another trick. We built a huge campfire on the gravel bar, hauling in driftwood from all directions. After dinner, and after drying out our wet gear, we kicked the coals around on top of the gravel. The embers warmed the gravel, and we unfolded the tent over that warmth. Slowly the heat came up through the tent. We fell asleep comfortably in our fluffed-up sleeping bags.

The next morning we set out downriver again. Seeing the open channels in the daylight, we were glad we had not gone farther in the dark. We pulled into Rohn Roadhouse, an official checkpoint, by mid-morning. I stayed for a cup of hot coffee while the other mushers took off for McGrath.

About noon I took off. For the first time on the race I traveled alone. Cabbage did wonderfully, sensing the invisible trail along the ice and through miles of slushy overflow. An afternoon all alone in the middle of that quiet country gave my spirit strength and peace. Several nights later, under a cloudy, windy sky, the little fish camp on the Salmon River appeared. A silent, dark cabin, a high cache, and a wall tent surrounded by several sleds and a few snow machines waited on the riverbank. Several dogs staked out in the willows barked a subdued welcome, but the rest just curled up tighter, cherishing their rest time and hoping the commotion wouldn't wake their masters. A lamp flickered through the window of the cabin and the soft light grew steadily. It was about three in the morning.

The Petruska family from Nikolai had offered their fish camp to be used as a checkpoint. The whole family moved to camp for the race. They welcomed every musher, no matter when the team arrived. Mr. Petruska invited me in to warm up and have a hot meal. I unharnessed my dogs and rummaged through the pile of supplies that had been flown in from McGrath. My gunnysack was there, tagged with the familiar handwriting. Years seemed to have passed since I was back in my friend's messy kitchen, melting tallow and mixing it with the vitamins and the hundreds of pounds of dog food. What a job it had been, pouring the glop into cardboard boxes which formed the bricks I was now chopping for the dogs.

My flashback ended abruptly as my fingers stiffened in the cold. I fed the dogs and knocked softly at the cabin door. A bowl of steaming stew sat on the table in front of the only empty chair in the cabin. We talked with hushed voices as small children shifted in their sleep. One older girl rocked her younger brother who had been awakened by the light. The hot food thawed my body and the tranquil family eased the tension that had accumulated with the frost.

The wall tent outside had room for one more sleeping bag. A dim flashlight glowed in the corner. I carefully pulled back the tent flap. Another musher was stuffing his sleeping bag in its sack. He motioned to tell me there was room in his corner. I stepped over the sleeping bodies and fluffed out my bag. The tent smelled sweet from the thick spruce boughs covering the snow, reminding me of childhood Christmas trees. I snuggled into my chilly bag and slowly warmed up, thinking nice Christmasy thoughts as I fell asleep. The sincere generosity of the Petruska family, like so many others along the trail, was like the Christmas spirit alive and very well in the middle of March.

Two days later my team pulled into McGrath. Schoolchildren jumped aboard on the outskirts of town and guided me to the checkpoint. I took my compulsory 24-hour layover there, and the six solid hours of sleep felt fantastic. Gladly I would have stayed a few more days, but my goal was to keep up with the other teams so I would make it all the way to Nome. If I lagged behind too far a blizzard might dump four feet of snow on the trail. Then I would find myself breaking trail on snowshoes alone and I needed help from the other mushers.

McGrath was a good place to regroup. I called a friend in Tanana to offer as slightly used sled dog. Thunder, one of the new recruits, had never pulled his fair share. I was tired of nagging him. With his long hair, I could see foot problems in the near future. The rest of my dogs were in good shape, except Ambler, who had a raw pad on his front left foot.

The veterinarian gave me some antibiotics, and I kept a dog bootie on him the rest of the trip. Some wonderful fans in Anchorage had sewn thousands of booties, and an ample supply was available at race headquarters. A special bundle had green cabbages decorated on them, and I kept a few for souvenirs. Luckily Ambler was the only dog on my team that needed to wear boots.

In McGrath I sent home a lot of the extra gear I was hauling: the wall tent, stove, stovepipe, and 20 pounds of stake-out chain. I had pitched the tent only one time so far, and its weight was not worth the comfort. I could sleep on my sled, but the way the race was speeding up, I wouldn't be sleeping much anyway. The dogs were so relieved to stop, a piece of thread would have held them. The teams traveling slower than I were dropping out of the race. This added pressure to push harder, just to stay up with the teams in front of me.

I pulled out of McGrath about midnight. Temperatures were uncomfortably warm in the daytime and night travel was easier on the dogs. Tony and I shared the dark miles together, pulling into Takotna around two in the morning. Even at that impossible hour we were called in for hot soup and good wishes for the trail.

By midafternoon the next day we were into the Ophir mining district. The race route left the trail to Flat and Iditarod and turned north following the rolling hills to Poorman. As our teams trotted through the seemingly deserted camp, a friendly "Yoo-hoo" beckoned us over to a small home.

Mr. and Mrs. Miskovich invited us in, their invitation reinforced by the irresistible aroma of fresh coffee. Homemade biscuits still warm from the oven awaited us. To sit in a real chair, at a real table, and look around at all the colorful treasures this woman had in her kitchen gave me a delightfully new perspective. I left Poorman a wealthy woman, rich with the warmth of two new friendships. That warmth kept me toasty all those 50 miles downhill to Ruby, jewel of the Yukon.

The Yukon River! I was halfway to Nome and the most difficult half was behind me. Dolly and Albert Yrjana opened their home to me in Ruby. I could have stayed weeks just to hear more of their stories of the early days in that little gold rush town, but the next morning I packed my sled, with Dolly and Albert twinkling, joking and wishing me well. In Albert's wonderful Finnish accent, he gave me some advice: "Every day, you learn something new on the Yukon." I repeated this farewell to myself many times in the next two hundred miles.

Around the wide curves of the Yukon to Galena, past Bishop Rock and Koyukuk, and along the bluffs leading to Nulato we went. Again I was traveling at night. About 10 miles upriver from Nulato, something surprised me along the trail. I dug out my flashlight and took a closer look. "Hot coffee ahead, keep on doggin'!" A few more miles down the trail, "The Nulato wolves are watching you!" From there on into the village, encouraging signs welcomed mushers every few miles. The school kids had created the posters and their messages had come at just the right time.

At Nulato I learned about the good-natured betting that was following the race. Most of the men had predicted that Lolly and I would scratch from the race in the first hundred miles. As we continued from checkpoint to checkpoint, the women were backing us and winning! I had a whole sledload of women riding along with me. That extra responsibility was fresh incentive to keep pushing.

The last stop on the Yukon River was the village of Kaltag. I was privileged to stay with Virginia and Edgar Kalland. Edgar had been one of the original Iditarod mushers who relayed the diphtheria serum to Nome. His memories of that trip gave life to the historic trail. He rummaged around the house and found his old wooden grub box which had ridden in his sled when he carried the mail between villages. He also brought out a pair of well-worn, beaded moose-hide mitts which Virginia had made for him many years before. The thrill of my visit with the Kallands boosted me up and over the Kaltag Portage, a 90-mile overland route cutting up from the Yukon over to Norton Sound.

A storm had drifted the trail on the eastern section. For the first time in the race I unlashed my snowshoes. Under the drifts the base of the old trail could be felt. For a while, all went well — slow, but well. A few other teams patiently waited behind me. After a mile or two I lost the base and went floundering in the deep snow. I made a 90° turn to my right and stamped off in a straight line till I returned to the old trail. After a short stretch the trail improved and the dogs went ahead on their own.

I reached the top of the pass about midnight. Three-thousand-foot peaks of the Kaltag Mountains bordered the broad crossing on each side. As if to help celebrate my arrival, the aurora began swirling around in skirts of green, yellow and red. I flopped onto my sled and craned my neck to watch the dance. That was the ideal spot in the world to watch the lights.

The next morning the gradual downhill run, following the broad valley of the Unalakleet River, carried me to the frozen sea. The gray-white pack ice of Norton Bay skirted the shore. Beyond that the sparkling promise of dark, deep water glistened in the sun. Never had my mushing horizon reached to the ocean. I was eager to try traveling on the frozen salt water.

At Unalakleet my friend from the University of Alaska, Agnes Baptise, treated me like a visiting queen. A steak dinner, a hot shower, and then a sweet night's sleep between clean sheets — what a contrast to restless nights curled up on the sled! Agnes rode with me down the shore ice the next morning. Before saying good-by, she gave me a pair of thick wool gloves her mom had knitted for me. It's surprising how a pair of beautiful gloves can warm your whole body and make you smile each time you look at them.

As I pulled into Shaktoolik, the next checkpoint, several other teams pulled out. When they were out of sight, the checker laughed and explained, "Now those fellas were going to stay the night and rest up their dogs. When they saw you coming they started rushing around, harnessing up. They sure didn't want no woman to pass them. Poor dogs — they were tired!"

"Well, I'm going to stay the night if it's O.K. with you," I said. "These dogs of mine deserve a little nap."

There were two reasons the sight of Lolly and me disturbed the other mushers. We were the first women to enter the Iditarod Race; that could be laughed off but here we were, still in it!

At Koyuk, the next checkpoint, the mushers' supplies were stored in the entryway to the school. I knew what to expect. In February I had scraped plates at the university dining hall. Selected leftovers were packed in plastic bags and quickly frozen in blocks to be divided along the way. Combined with the pemmican (the tallow, dog food and vitamin mixture) this diet proved satisfactory — with one exception, the broccoli. Bright green tidbits marked my campsites. I suspect some adventurous raven enjoyed the delicacies.

At Elim, a captivating village overlooking Norton Sound, the real push to Nome began. Elim was also the end of any real sleeping. Almost half of the teams that had started the race had dropped out or had been disqualified for dropping below the minimum-size team of five dogs. My original six dogs were doing fine. My seventh dog, the other new recruit, was just running in place, adding no pulling power.

Lolly Medley was covering the same daily distance that I was. She would spend longer hours on the trail, traveling at a slower speed, but always reached the same checkpoint within the 24-hour period. I would leave a few hours after her, meet her on the trail, stop for a chat or a cup of tea, and then continue to the next point. My dogs and I would snatch a few hours' rest, just enough to take us on for the next stretch. Lolly would arrive, maybe rest a few minutes, maybe just keep on going. I don't know how she could stay awake so long.

I surely did admire her determination. I felt so exhausted and groggy, just keeping my eyes open was an effort. Some competitive impulse surfaced and I decided I wanted to get to Nome before Lolly. My loyal team had worked so hard I owed it to them to finish as well as possible. So went my rationalization. There were only three teams behind me, but I wanted to keep it that way.

After a short rest in Elim we headed over the high hills to crash down to Golovin Bay. Cabbage sighted a light from the village and held course as best he could on the windswept ice. The gusting wind would catch the sled broadside and whip it up in front of the dogs, dragging them along with it. Little patches of snow would catch the runners, and everything would straighten out again, quite abruptly. A quick cup of coffee in Golovin and on to White Mountain with the sunrise, for breakfast with a wonderful Eskimo family fathered by Tom Brown. Then, in a sleepy fog, on over the hills to Solomon.

I reached the coast in the late afternoon light. As we came down the bluffs the darker blue of the open water glittered beyond the pack ice. Along the beach the wind roared over me. Few hints of the trail remained. Sculptures of dog footprints were preserved on two-foot-high pedestals. The soft snow that had not been pressed beneath the paws had blown away. The amazing footprints astounded both the dogs and me.

The driftwood, blown in during a late autumn storm, also seemed foreign. Things were changing — the country and the feeling about it all. It was the beginning of the end. The dogs seemed to sense the new urgency.

We reached Solomon, the last checkpoint before Nome, just as the sun was sinking into the ocean. The checker, kept up to date by Nome radio broadcasts, predicted that Lolly would arrive within two hours, but the other teams were a good day behind us.

When Lolly arrived, we enjoyed a delicious spaghetti and meatball dinner. Since there was no team close behind us, Lolly and I decided to take a rest. At least that was my understanding, but maybe I hadn't been listening well. When I awoke several hours later Lolly was no longer in the other bed, but on her way to Nome. I harnessed up and took chase. I always had passed her before and surely I could do it again. But with only 20 more miles to go, did I have time?

I urged my team on with a new compelling tone in my voice. "Come on, Cabbage, one more dash and you can sleep for a day. Take me home to Nome. Take me as fast as you can! Come on, Kiana! Hit it, Ole!" The dogs picked it up, and we zoomed along under the clear starry sky.

The trail followed a summer road, with mileposts marking the distance. With only 10 miles left I was worried and mad. I could not see Lolly's head lamp. She must be far ahead. Just then the dogs bunched up, confused as to where the trail went.

Lights were moving along the road to my right, so I "geeed" Cabbage up the bank toward them. From this elevation I saw the lights of Nome for the first time, only three or four miles away. The road was gravelly, creating a drag on the runners. The dogs were straining and I ran along behind to lighten the load.

A group of vehicle lights seemed to move together about a mile in front of me. That must be Lolly's escort, I told myself. If she's only a mile ahead, I still have a chance. We've passed her every other time, it's only fair we pass her now. "Come on you mutts, race!"

But they couldn't. The car lights stayed ahead of us. I had to try something else. I "hawed" my dogs over the steep bluff to the sea ice. It was dark, but perhaps I would find a faster trail down there. I zigzagged my way around driftwood and over what sounded like exposed sand. I didn't use a head lamp, so I couldn't see for sure. The dogs were doing their best but my plan wasn't working. The trail wasn't any faster on the ice. I "geeed" the team back up to the road.

When the front dogs gained the road level, they surprised some race fans who were sitting in a car, their radio tuned into the race coverage.

"Hey! There's Lolly right in front of us. That must be Mary's head lamp out on the trail," someone said. "Congratulations, Lolly! You're the first woman to finish the Iditarod! Mary's still a couple of miles behind you. You've only got a mile more to go now."

I looked out the trail. Sure enough, I could see a faint light slowly moving through the darkness. "Are you sure Lolly isn't up in front of me?" I asked.

"What do you mean? Aren't you Lolly? The radio said Lolly was first out of Solomon and you're the first team to come along. Who are you anyway?" they asked, excitedly.

"I'm Mary Shields. I better keep on going. Thanks for the information. That's the best news I've heard all night!"

I released the brake and my team trotted off. We headed back down to the ice for the second time. The dogs swerved sharply to the right as they picked up a well-used trail. I relaxed and let them set their own pace. The dogs understood that pulling into this checkpoint was going to be different. They trotted along eagerly, curious to see if my promise of The End would hold true. I was relieved to be there, too, and a little sad.

In minutes we reached the turn going up to Front Street. A little Eskimo lady waited under the first street light. She stuck out her arm and stuffed a small package into my kuspuk pocket. I thanked her and kept going. The sirens were screaming, signaling people of my arrival. It was about four o'clock in the morning.

The street was partitioned off with a snow fence. The finish line waited at the end of the center lane. The whole community of Nome seemed to be lining the fence, cheering me on, welcoming me to their town. My dogs were a little frightened by the noise and the flash bulbs.

I ran up alongside the team, talking softly to my bewildered companions, "It's O.K., Kiana. You're doing just fine. Cabbage, you keep 'em moving right over that line. You're the best lead dog in the whole wide world."

The finish line was only a hundred feet in front of us. Cabbage, Kiana, Ole, Kobuk, Ambler, Luna and Snowflake trotted along, pulling the sled the last steps of the 1,049-mile journey. About 30 women, bundled in their parkas and kuspuks, stretched across the finish line holding a banner over their heads: "You've Come a Long Way, Baby!"

They separated to let us pass through the center. The roar from the crowd thundered to the stars. All of Nome was there to celebrate, especially Nome's women.

As the dogs crossed the line, they were scooped up into the bed of a pickup truck. I pushed my way through the crowd of officials to see what they were doing with my dogs. That team had been with me nearly every minute of the last 28 days and nights and they were not going to disappear now. They deserved the real welcome, the real reward.

The race committee assured me the dogs would be made comfortable at the airport. All the finishing teams were kept there. I could go visit them in the morning. I gave each dog a hug and a thank-you and let them go. The mob gently pushed me over to a platform. The mayor's wife officially welcomed me. An

FINISH LINE

YOU'VE COME A LONG WAY, BABY!

Illustration by Sharon Schumacher

armful of red roses was pushed under my nose, and I breathed in their sweetness as if I had never smelled roses before. The disk jockey's wife interviewed me over the radio. A bottle of champagne was stuck under my other arm.

Twenty teams already had come over that line, but still Nome had heart enough to open up for me. Everyone was celebrating; many had started early. The women seemed especially happy, and I was one of the happiest.

I wandered around race headquarters and found a cup of hot cocoa. About a half-hour later, the sirens cried out again. The crowds rushed out, and the finish chute brightened with flash bulbs and cheers. I wiggled in and joined the jubilant crowd welcoming Lolly Medley. She was all smiles, her head lamp pushed back on her forehead, her big parka unzipped over her snow-go suit. She whistled and cooed to her dogs as they steadily trotted over the line. The crowd boomed and the banner waved high above. More roses and welcomes. The town started celebrating anew.

Nome has a way of treating every team that finishes as though it were the winner. That welcome is a memory dear to the heart. Lolly and I were given the fanciest suite at the Nome Inn for as long as we wanted to stay in town. Baskets of fresh fruit sat on the dressers. More fresh flowers and champagne waited in the bedroom. I drew a hot bath and settled in the steamy deep tub. Layers of frostbitten skin peeled from my cheeks. When I awoke the water was cool. I added more hot water and tried to regain some life.

I had my blue journal next to the tub, the journal I had been going to keep faithfully along the trip. On page one I made my very first entry: "April 1, 1974 — in the bathtub in Nome — well— you've come a long way baby!!! Not too much time for writing, but what a wonderful trip! Good dogs, good friends. My way works."

Again I fell asleep in the tub. Later I got out and climbed in between clean sheets. For an instant I reveled in the luxury. Then I slept, no doubt a smile on my face.

The next morning I started walking out to the airport. After being part of a sled, part of a team, for nearly a month, I felt strange moving along by myself, and an odd sort of loneliness. The third car to pass me gave me a lift.

At the airport, tethered on a long stake-out chain, my seven sleeping dogs were curled up on pieces of cardboard. "Hello, good friends!" I greeted them. Seven balls of fur expanded into wiggly, waggly happy dogs. Hugs and scratches for each, and then they were unsnapped for a little romp. I congratulated them and flattered them and teased them and praised them. I was very proud of that little team.

I pulled the sled over so Cabbage could curl up on the caribou hide in the basket. He jumped aboard, curled up and looked content to sleep another year or two. I rounded up more cardboard for the rest of the dogs. When they all seemed comfortable I returned to Nome.

Back in the hotel I sorted through my gear to find something to wear while my only complete set of clothes was being washed. A resident of Nome had volunteered to take the dirties home and return them fresh and clean. Going through the pockets of my kuspuk, I found the little package — a round leather picture of a dog team racing along in front of some mountains, with the thin moon watching above. It was all handmade out of brown, white and black calfskin.

A little note explained the gift: "My dear lady, I hear you are the first woman to come in that race they are having. I just wish to make you happy, so I give you this picture. Your friend, Helen Sanugatuk." The precious gift, and the kind thought that went with it, represented the warmth given me by the entire city of Nome. I felt very privileged to know this generosity.

In the afternoon the last two teams came in. Red Olson and Joel Kottke proclaimed The End, each with half of the message written on a paper-plate poster. Again the city came out with a grand welcome. These two mushers received the honor they deserved.

That night the second mushers' banquet was held. (The first half of the finishers celebrated a week earlier.) I skipped out to the kitchen, complimented the cook on the delicious meal, and asked if the scraps were available.

The cook smiled and said, "Come back in an hour." A heaping bucket was waiting when I returned. The dogs had their own little banquet the next day. There was also a note from the cook. "Mary, if you're interested in running the race next year, I'd be interested in sponsoring you." Pretty nice offer.

Two days in Nome were enough for me. A letter from John reported melting snow back in the Interior. I reread that several times. Hmmmm, I said to myself, the trail here is perfect. Why rush back to breakup?

My cheeks were raw from frostbite and I was still hacking from the "walking pneumonia", a souvenir most mushers had from the Ptarmigan Pass weather; but overall I felt wonderful, physically strong and mentally alert.

I went to the airport and talked things over with the team. They were agreeable so I harnessed up. We turned down onto the ice to backtrack along the Iditarod.

Chapter 6
The Long Way Back

HOW DIFFERENT the trail looked in the bright daylight. The sun was rolling high toward its summer path and the reflection off the ice and snow doubled its brilliance and warmth, lining my face with squinting eyes and a spontaneous smile. The temperature relaxed around zero.

After traveling only five miles from Nome I swung my team into the deep snow and stopped for one last look, one last memory. I poured a hot cup of tea and stretched out on top of my sled. My eyes climbed the slope from the sea ice up to the road. Only a few nights before I had become competitive on that slope. I had been confused, but in the daylight my mistakes seemed careless.

Where had I crashed down looking for the trail? Where had I passed Lolly in the dark? The tracks would keep their secret under the windswept snow. The warm sun soothed any concern about it and I closed my eyes. I let myself drift away and the dogs followed my example, sprawling out on the snow, a sleepy head rested on a partner's back.

A few hours later I awoke with a chill. I fooled around with the dogs, scratching, teasing and sweet-talking to them. They seemed to have enjoyed their nap. Their enthusiasm was a welcome change from the exhaustion of the weeks before.

We continued past Solomon, along the coast toward the east. The setting sun, dropping off into the ocean, highlighted the rusty bluffs we were climbing. The beauty of the scene erased all thoughts of the race and, for the first time in nearly a month, I could concentrate on the world around me. I said farewell to the ocean, slipped over the crest of the bluff and glided down the rolling hills toward White Mountain. The trail was smooth and well packed. The treeless hills parted peacefully to let us pass.

The next day we rounded the bend in the Indian River and pulled up into White Mountain, a friendly cluster of about 25 weathered cabins. I visited with the Tom Brown family, my hosts of the week before. Tom talked with a quiet voice. His cloudy eyes had seen more of life than most of us. His words were chosen kindly and wisely.

A tantalizing pot of reindeer stew was taken off the wood cookstove and placed in the center of the table. The aroma silently signaled the family which appeared from all directions — children, teen-agers and elders. Some neighbors popped in during the meal, anxious to report on their successful grizzly bear hunt. A little Eskimo lady had done the shooting. Her husband was very proud of her. He explained her name in Eskimo was *Mik-chrok Ah-nak Chup-pnng-nak-toka*. Translated into English, it meant "Small-but-oh-my!"

Later that afternoon, as my team headed downriver toward Golovin, I promised myself I would name a female pup after her, but already I had forgotten how to pronounce it. I made up a little song to remember it as we slipped along the smooth trail.

My dogs eagerly pulled up the bank to Elim. A lady came out and invited me to stay at her home. We found a good place for the dogs and then joined her husband inside for a cup of tea and some pilot crackers spread with shortening. Ralph and Betty were full of race talk. I answered their questions and they answered mine. After many hours of visiting, Betty asked me to join them on a short day trip to the village hot springs. I was honored and delighted.

The next morning they packed me on the snow-go sled. Betty stood on the runners behind me, and Ralph pulled us along behind his bright yellow machine. I felt like the Queen of Sheba, although as we roared past my dogs I hoped they wouldn't see me. Cabbage gave a suspicious glance our way, but the rest of the team was content to sleep the day away, each dog comfortably curled up on the little spruce-bough nest the kids had gathered for them.

The hot springs flowed in a little algae-covered stream. The pool was dammed up with a row of big rocks, providing room for several persons. The trapped water deepened to about four feet and the temperature was perfect, about the same as a very hot bath. As Betty and I floated in the pool, I gazed out at the surrounding snowy mountains and felt superbly clean and refreshed. The sharing of this natural wonder was something I will always cherish.

The miles slipped away gently as I left Elim that afternoon, heading straight across the pack ice for Shaktoolik rather than retracing the trail up around the north bay near Koyuk. A strong wind was blowing in my face and my long wool scarf was whipping over my shoulder. I stopped the team to retie the scarf, turning my back to the gusts so I could adjust the folds over my tender, frostbitten cheeks.

My bulky mittens hindered my hands, and the wind blowing

the scarf didn't help at all. Being miles out of earshot of anyone else, I felt free to give the scarf a good piece of my mind, rather loudly. Several minutes later I was all bundled up again. I turned around and lifted my foot to step back onto the sled runner.

That was a step I could not reach, because the sled and team were half a mile ahead of me. All my fussing and hollering at the scarf must have been taken as a command to take off. The dogs were moving right along, no doubt enjoying the lightened load. I yelled into the wind at them, but my words whistled back over my shoulder, just as the scarf had. There I stood, alone in the middle of the pack ice.

About then Cabbage must have caught a glimpse of me, for he swung the team around and they came galloping back even faster than they had left. As I knelt on the snow in the middle of the trail, the whole team plowed in for hugs and wags and wiggles. I spent the next 10 minutes untangling the spaghetti of tug lines and towlines, but I was happy to have the whole mess back around me.

That night we camped halfway across the bay. The dogs slept in harness, tethered on neck lines or tug lines. I pulled the sled up alongside the dogs and fluffed out my sleeping bag. At the very moment the orange ball of the sun rolled off the western edge of the ice, a rosy full moon eased up on the southeastern edge, balancing the loss in the sky. I lay in my sleeping bag, pondering the wonder of ice, sky, sun and moon. The faint, shy stars slowly gained confidence as the night darkened. I fell asleep with a twinkling peace.

Returning to Unalakleet, I again stayed with my friend Agnes. She took me around the village to visit her friends and relatives. Everywhere we went people encouraged me to make a side trip to visit Frank and Eunice Ryan. So of course I headed out the trail for the visit, a huge box of fried chicken, a gift from Agnes to the

Ryans, tucked in my sled. As their cabin came in view an outburst of excited barking announced my arrival. Frank, a short, gray-haired man in his late 60s, came out to investigate the commotion. He helped me tie down my sled and then took me to see his dogs.

"Someday these dogs will make a good Iditarod team for Eunice. We only keep the white pups from each litter. Her team will be all white huskies, faster than the wind," Frank proudly explained.

Eunice, appearing to be in her mid-30s, came out and invited us in for tea. She was just finishing the dishes, carefully stacking them to dry in the warm cookstove oven, leaving the door open. On the wall of the small cabin hung Bill Berry's wildlife map of Alaska, bordered by a handmade, white birch frame. (Bill was a friend of mine back in Fairbanks, and I reminded myself to tell him of this most appropriate setting for his map.) I presented the box of chicken, but, before I could identify the giver, the Ryans were laughing and praising Agnes's cooking.

We talked about the race. Frank reminisced about his life in Unalakleet and the days of the great reindeer herds. Then he jumped to his mushing days, back when he had hauled mail over the Kaltag portage to the Yukon. He knew by heart the trail that lay ahead of me and mentioned tricky places of the past.

After a few hours I headed for the trail again. Frank came out to give my dogs a treat. From his fish cache he brought seven shiny, frozen trout, caught in the Unalakleet River. He gave each dog the gift. They chomped and gulped until the delicacies were gone. We said good-by again and my satisfied dogs trotted out with fresh enthusiasm.

The Kaltag portage was even more spectacular than I remembered. With a clear mind and a rested body, I could really appreciate the country. The trail was pretty good as there had been considerable snow-go traffic since the race. At one place I recognized an old campfire spot Tony and I had used. A glint of dark steel caught my eye. I kicked off the snow and there was the knife Tony had lost. I tucked it into my sled bag, to return to Tony when I got home.

A few miles later Cabbage veered off the trail, pulling Kiana into the deep snow. I didn't understand what he was doing — the trail ahead was good. I commanded him back to the trail, and he reluctantly returned. Twenty yards farther along things began to make sense.

I could see a faint trail connecting off to the left, where Cab had been aiming. When we had come through here on the race the trail had been drifted over. I had snowshoed ahead trying to feel the trail and keep us on it. At one point I got off into the deep snow, floundered for a while and finally turned to my right and went in a straight line until I felt the packed trail under my snowshoes. Then I continued on the trail.

Cabbage just wanted to return exactly as he had come, every step of the way. In a million years I couldn't have recognized that drifted-over jog in the trail, but Cabbage was a one-in-a-million dog.

In Kaltag I visited the Kallands again. Virginia took me around the village to meet her friends. I was given a pair of bright blue gloves made by the Kaltag Women's Club. My warm fingers warmed my heart whenever I remembered their kindness.

Traveling up the Yukon, I took advantage of the cooler night-time temperatures when the trail hardened up after the day's thaw. This schedule also allowed me to take advantage of the warm sunshine. I slept comfortably on top of my sled while the dogs basked in the sunny snow. The Iditarod checkers gave me leftover dog food, so the sledload was light and the dogs were well fed.

Many villages were celebrating with their spring carnivals. Traffic up and down the river was continual, packing the trail like a highway. On April 15, exactly two weeks after I left Nome, I reached Galena, about five hundred miles back toward Fairbanks. The snow was up to some serious melting those last days. The trail just barely set up under the full moon. Galena was the last stop where I could fly home without chartering a plane on my own. The reality of breakup and my remaining funds told me it was time to take to the air.

Cabbage and Kiana turned up the bank of the Yukon and headed directly for the airport. The long air force landing field was quiet, not a plane in sight, so we headed straight across.

Suddenly sirens were whining and a voice was booming over a loudspeaker, "Stop right where you are. Turn around and go back across the runway. Report directly to the commander's office."

Armed guards with real guns took defensive stands in front of me. I did a "Come-gee" and under my breath I told Cabbage, "Well, old buddy , I guess we've come to the end of the trail. After fifteen hundred miles of snow, wind and cold, the U.S. government is making us turn back. Somehow I can't take them too seriously."

I reported to the commanding officer and pleaded innocent. He was still pretty upset, but with nothing to lose, I asked about hitching a ride home on an empty military plane. The officer didn't like my idea, so we said good-by. On to the Wien Airlines counter I went.

I had inquired about flight arrangements while I was still in Nome. The agent there assured me I could rent an igloo, a huge plastic cargo container, to hold all my dogs and the sled. The special musher's rate for the package was reasonable, and I had budgeted for it. Unfortunately, the Galena agent could only refer to his regulation book, which required me to purchase a cage for each dog. The sled would go separately. This all amounted to about 10 times more money and I was in a fix.

Just then a Galena man, overhearing my predicament, came up and offered me the loan of his son's dog box. I gratefully accepted Mr. Huntington's offer and congratulated him on Carl's victory in Nome. Carl Huntington was the 1974 Iditarod champ.

The four-by-six-foot crate was loaded on the waiting plane. I ran the dogs up to the belly of the aircraft. The freight handlers helped the dogs into the plane, and then all together we stuffed the seven into the crate and lowered the plywood lid, weighting it down with the dog sled on top. Faithful eyes peered out of the breathing holes. After all the strange experiences those dogs had gone through they weren't too upset.

I boarded the passenger section of the plane directly behind the freight compartment, separated only by a thin partition which was moved forward or backward to make room for more freight or more passengers depending on the day's demands. As the plane rumbled down the runway, one final good-by howl rose from my companions on the other side of the partition.

I pressed my forehead to the window and watched Galena, the Yukon River and the Iditarod Trail fall away into the past. Those old butterfly tears fluttered down my cheeks again, but their wings were bright and strong. I said my own good-by to the greatest adventure that, so far in my life, I had ever had.

Chapter 7
"Framed a house of moss and timber,
called it a home."
—John Haines

HOME — a familiar corner of the world, a center for the wanderers to return to. There is a pleasure in returning along the home trail, of knowing every bump and bend, every root and low branch, of returning in the dark as comfortably as an owl landing in the branches of a spruce on a moonless night.

When I returned from the Iditarod, there was no tall friend waiting at the airport to greet me, but a note pinned on the door of my little shack read, "Welcome back, M.! I'm out at the creek, cutting logs for the cabin. Come out as soon as you can. Love, J."

I joined John in a few days. The events of the previous six weeks bubbled up. John had been freighting supplies for John Bryant's Mount McKinley expedition and told stories of mushing through McGonagall Pass and of the bottomless crevasses that severed the trail. But there would be other seasons for mountain mushing. It was April and there was dog work waiting right there in the creek bottom.

John had carefully selected 50 trees to use for the cabin. He measured the circumference with a string, matching logs with a near 8-inch diameter about three feet up from the ground. With a lot of help from our friend Bob James, a living superman, the trees were felled, limbed and dragged to several piles along the creek.

My part, with the able assistance of my furry friends, was to move the logs uphill a quarter-mile to the building site. The 70 longest ones, 25 feet, were green and heavy, weighing several hundred pounds each. Without the help of the dogs our home in the woods would still be "in the woods."

John built a sturdy little sledge for the job, which we nicknamed the log-dogger. I ran the team to the log pile, did a "Come-haw," and loaded the log butt end first, with the lighter tail end dragging behind. A timber hitch held the log on the sledge. With the command to "Hike" the dogs took off and I stepped out of the way. After their initial burst of energy the dogs settled down to a pace I could keep up with. I helped steer the sledge around trees and pushed on the uphills. The log was unloaded at the building site.

The hard part of the trip was over for the dogs. The hard part for me was just beginning. Returning downhill to the log pile without a brake was a real test of my dogs' training. On the first run of the day I would start back with just three dogs, two of them attached only by their neck lines so they couldn't pull so hard. John would let loose two other dogs when I signaled from the log pile. By afternoon the dogs were bored and tired enough that I could go down with a full team.

We hauled four or five loads a day. Between trips, I peeled the bark off the logs with a drawknife. By working steadily, I kept John supplied. On May 9 the last log arrived on the site. The team was retired for the season and they lounged away the days in the warm sun, watching us work on the cabin. We fitted the last roof pole on May 15 and returned to Fairbanks for summer jobs. A midsummer return trip completed the sod roof.

The next fall, we finished the windows and door and prepared for winter. But a log cabin isn't a home until it warms you with a crackling fire. With the first snowfall the dogs had another important errand to run.

The fire would burn in a five-hundred-pound cast-iron cook range. John built an extra-heavy-duty sledge to carry the stove, with the warming ovens and water reservoir dismantled to make the load more compact. We planned to pop popcorn as we moved it along the trail, but the cold temperature kept us too busy to pop. The stove made the trip in good shape, tipping over only once on an icy creek about 12 miles out the trail.

Now that the cabin home was complete, we started on log doghouses for the team. "Doggie-duplexes," sharing a common wall, required the fewest number of logs and notches. Sheets of plywood were hauled in to make waterproof roofs. Huge bundles of tall dry grass along the creek were cut to be used for bedding. The dogs loved the sweet smell. They wiggled in, stomping around till they had acceptable nests padded down.

The dogs made living at the cabin possible. A home off the beaten path meant breaking trail to get there, and hauling in supplies on our backs would have limited our stays. Having the dogs' help inspired us to dream of living at the creek more of the year, perhaps even permanently.

"You know," John said, "it's silly for both of us to cut wood for our two cabins back in town. If you moved in with me, we could cut one supply, together."

"Interesting possibility," I agreed, admitting to myself that this was not the first time I had considered the idea, although not exactly in terms of firewood.

Chapter 8
Go Where There Is No Trail

THE PLANS WERE MADE. For our 1976 spring trip we would visit friends living at Lake Minchumina. Then a letter came offering me a six-week substitute teaching job at Ruby. (Pat Sweetsir, the regular teacher, was going to Fairbanks to have her fifth baby.) The job sounded great — and why not get to it by dog team?

The trip to Lake Minchumina would cover about four hundred miles. To continue to Ruby, on the Yukon River, would more than double our distance, expanding the trip to approximately a thousand miles. We also would have to go earlier than we had originally planned, because I was to begin teaching March 15. John and I talked it over, agreed on the adventure, and gathered a few more maps.

Blessed with splendid weather, we departed McKinley Park headquarters on February 15. The sky was clear and the temperature was an unseasonably warm -10° F. "What have we done to deserve such wonderful weather?" I asked John.

"We're just living right," he answered, tucking his extra mittens in his sled bag.

The trail through the park was excellent, thanks to the National Park Service's dog patrol and Dennis Kogl's Denali Dog Tours. These first 50 miles were a real treat. We daydreamed of the bygone days when extensive trails connected communities all over Alaska and were mainly kept open by the mail carriers.

We first caught a glimpse of McKinley when it was still 90 miles in the distance. Throughout the rest of our journey our perspective would change and we would measure our movement in relationship to this prominent center. Again I felt protected, back in the view of the High One.

From the Toklat River west we were breaking our own trail, but lucky stars, the wind, and previous years' passings prepared our way. No more turning north to Wonder Lake this year, but on past the Clearwater, on past the Muddy. When I realized we were moving into new country, an overpowering exhilaration exploded in me. I dramatically recited some favorite lines I had left pinned over the cabin door. The lines were by Knud Rasmussen, the arctic explorer.

> *Only the Air-Spirits know*
> *what lies beyond the hills;*
> *Yet I urge my team farther on.*
> *Drive on and on, on and on!*

Certainly this was no polar expedition, just the beginning of our own little adventure, but we felt wonderful to be on our way!

On the last sunny bend before entering the shady Eagle Gorge, we stopped for lunch and hot tea. I warmed my hands in Cabbage's black fur, which had trapped the morning's sunlight.

John and I joked about the advantages of having a Labrador for a leader, considering the questionable river ice which lay ahead. I was getting a little nervous, even imagining I could hear running water.

We had been warned by other mushers and pilots not to try the gorge. I reconsidered our judgment in ignoring these warnings. After all, the entire north-facing drainage of the Alaska Range, from Stony Divide west to the park boundary, some four hundred square miles, was funneling through this 50-foot channel. According to the land, this was the best route for the water. According to our map, it was also the most direct route for us. We'd never know whether to chance it until we tried.

The walls rose up a hundred feet on both sides, as we entered the narrow gorge. I turned to McKinley for a little encouragement, but I could no longer see the sparkling guardian. I wondered if the spell still held in the shadowy canyon.

The sound of rushing water splashed by in reality as we made the second bend. Along the bluff's edge, the shelf ice held for about three feet, then it opened in a two-inch crack and sloped down to the water at a 30° angle. We concentrated on that shore edge, trying to ignore the rolling water just five feet to the left. Sometimes huge boulders appeared, perhaps 10 feet tall, completely covered by the turbulent clear water. Scenes of dogs, sleds and mushers being swept into the water flashed through my mind. Even the dogs seemed a little nervous.

Sometimes we deliberately hooked a sled runner in the crack, to help keep the sled from dragging the dogs down the slanting ice. My brand-new sled, which John had completed just the day before we left, suffered a few battle scars when I flipped it on its side to act as an anchor. This trick saved the whole works several times, so I considered the scars a reasonable price to pay for safe passage.

About halfway through the canyon, we took a break and John climbed around on the bright chartreuse rocks. We both were interested in the lichens that grew on the walls, and this green one was new to us. John stuffed a sample in his pocket. Later we sent the bright mystery to a botanist friend, Dr. James Anderson, at the University of Alaska. He informed us that our sample was not a lichen at all. It was a bright mineral outcropping, arsenal pyrite, containing sulfur, which produced sulfuric acid when combined with water. This information explained what happened to John's pocket. Little crumbs that remained there had mixed with the melting snow, forming acid which destroyed the entire bottom seam of his pocket and parka. I patched the seam and our botanical curiosity survived the acid test.

Just when we expected the gorge to end the shelf ice narrowed to less than a foot. I remained with the two teams as John walked ahead to scout out a safe route. After he disappeared around the curve, I realized I could not see or hear him if he needed help. It seemed as though he was gone for hours and I wanted to advance just far enough to keep him in view. There was nothing to tie the sleds to though, and I knew the dogs would try to follow as soon as I disappeared. Our job was to wait and be patient.

At last John returned, and the dogs whined and wagged their relief. I was whining and wagging inside myself, but I tried to appear calm and confident on the surface. We'd talked about the danger involved on these trips and we had both agreed the reward was worth the risk. The challenge of the unexpected sometimes forced us beyond our seeming limits, but this new territory was a refreshing place to visit.

John's scouting found no safe route ahead. We would have to cross to the other side where the shelf ice looked continuous. We backtracked until we found a safe crossing, keeping a respectable distance between the two teams, to spread out the weight. John started across the main channel. When his team reached the safety of the far side, I followed, bursting the silence with a whoop of celebration. We continued and the gorge snaked on endlessly. This was no place to be traveling in the dark.

We searched each bend for a safety island large enough to hold the five-by-seven-foot wall tent. Our standards lowered with each curve. Just in the last-chance moments of twilight we came upon a small bench gently sloping to the ice.

Black spruce seedlings had found this sanctuary two hundred years ago. With some careful hunting we gathered enough dead snags for firewood. We snowshoed a sleeping platform, building up the downhill side with surplus snow from uphill. We weren't very particular that night. The country had been more than hospitable in allowing us passage where neither boat nor foot could follow. Now a warm, safe campsite; time to rest, refuel and remember.

My sleepy mind thought of ancient snows that fell before man ever wandered the narrow land bridge connecting the two northern continents. How that pristine snow must have sparkled on McKinley's summit. A mountain wind raged, carrying the snow to the Muldrow Basin below. Years of accumulation followed, pressing the snow into ice. As the environment warmed, the weight and pressure of the glacier freed the snow, sending it down the great blue ice tunnels to the river flowing below. Now, 150 miles downstream, more of that water was gurgling past our tent, a Pleistocene lullaby linking us with the past.

On the water would flow, down the McKinley River, the Kantishna, the Tanana, and the mighty Yukon, on to the Pacific, to return with the next tide. The river was like a long winding root, part of the mountain reaching out across the land. This root carried water away, and millions of smaller roots drank the water, temporarily interrupting its long journey. I was one of those thirsty roots. My sleepy dreams flowed on with the watery lullaby.

The next morning we continued, the shelf ice holding well. After a few hours' travel we rounded a sharp bend, and the river opened to a half-mile-wide, braided valley. As we moved out into the sunshine, the tension melted away. Almost unconsciously, I glanced back over my left shoulder. There was McKinley, keeping watch as promised, long snow plumes racing off the summit. I "yahoooed" my dogs to a gallop, nodding a sincere wink of appreciation to the High One.

Traveling down the McKinley River was pure pleasure. The dogs could break trail through the snowy stretches. As we got farther away from the gorge, the snow was transformed by overflow ice. That year we had three pups along: Oscar, Melozie and Bimbo; each new experience was traumatic for them, yet entertaining for us. They were sons of Luna, our only female. They had the tall strong build we were looking for and this trip would be their chance to prove themselves.

Five miles down the McKinley River we encountered our first bare ice. Oscar was overwhelmed. His legs slipped out in four directions. His neck line dragged him, helping him to right himself. He padded along for a few steps, only to capsize again. With all the concentration a young dog can muster, his face wrinkled up with worry, Oscar studied the ice and tried to keep up. His ears drooped and his tail curled under his belly. He carried his body close to the ice, either to lower his center of gravity or just to shorten the distance of the inevitable fall. But, slowly, over

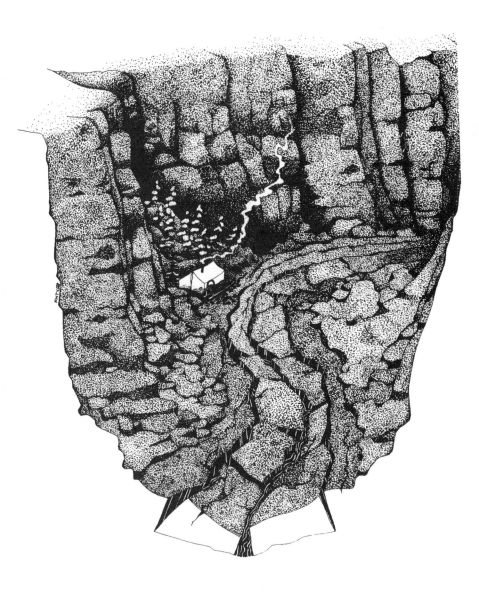

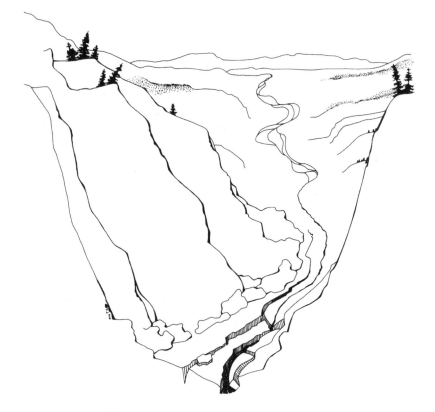

the miles, he gained confidence. His toenails dug in, trusting the slightly rough texture of the ice. At last Oscar learned to depend on the tension of his tug line for stability.

Just as this condition was mastered, we moved into a stretch of slushy overflow. Melozie, Oscar's partner in "wheel" (directly before the sled), tried to put on the brakes. The rest of the team ignored his efforts. He found himself dragging through the three inches of water in a sitting position. This was more disagreeable than walking through it so, with a nudge from the brush bow, Melozie joined the march, shaking each paw to rid himself of the danger. When this didn't work, he broke into a gallop, trying to escape the endless puddle. Again the rest of the team ignored his efforts and his gallop spun like a wheel on ice.

As the miles slipped beneath us we moved into yet another ice condition. This was smooth glare ice, freshly frozen the night before. There was absolutely no texture. The heavy sleds became weightless, meeting no resistance from the flawless surface. The dogs adjusted their gait, enjoying the easier job — all except Morgan, John's notorious 20-mile-an-hour lead dog.

Morgan had no power to stand up on the ice. He had at least 10 years of experience, so, when even the pups were managing, we couldn't understand his problem. John went up and carefully stood his faithful lead dog on his feet. As soon as John let go of the harness, the panicky dog crashed to the ice.

From my view, Morgan looked like a puppet, only able to act as sled dog when John pulled the strings. As John's patience shrank, Morgan's frustration grew. We put my team up in front. With this extra incentive Morgan finally got his team moving, interrupted by an uncontrollable belly flop every now and then.

Bimbo, John's pup, found another mystery in this clear ice. Huge air bubbles, trapped en route to the surface, were visible for several feet below. Wide-eyed Bimbo was spooked by these bubbles. At first he just pulled off to the side in a wide arc, trying to avoid them. When he crossed another bubble Bimbo arched his back and leaped over it, springing as high as his harness would allow. These repeated detours added little to our progress, so John decided to try a little pup psychology.

He gathered up the 90 pounds of struggling pup, determined to plunk him down on top of a bubble. Bimbo would learn that the bubble was harmless and the problem would be solved. That was the plan. However, Bimbo scrambled with all his considerable might and John smashed down to get a close-up view of the bubble himself. To make matters worse, Bimbo, in his attempts to escape, nearly ran over John with the heavy sled. The pups would have to learn by themselves. They did, and later in the trip when they had mastered the trials of the trail, I missed their curious antics. Our canine clowns had become seasoned troopers.

As we turned onto the Kantishna River we immediately hit deep overflow. The basket of the sled rippled through the water and darkness forced us to think of a campsite. Just then a whiff of wood smoke swirled through the air. We followed the sweet promise to a little cabin on the high bank. We ran the dogs up out of the water and tipped our sleds on to their sides. Walking up to the door, we "Helloed" and "Anybody-home?" but there was no answer. A radio was blaring and lamplight brightened the window. Finally we cracked the door a bit. A surprised old-timer motioned us in, blinking and rubbing his eyes, trying to decide if we were real or just part of his interrupted dream. We answered his questions as he checked us over with puzzled eyes, verifying the dogs through the window.

After a pot of hot coffee, we were ready to be on our way. When Al Starr invited us to stay the night, we were happy not to have to pitch camp in the dark. We shared dinner. Just as Al was warming up to the idea of having company, we became drowsy from the warmth of the cabin.

I can't remember Al blowing out the lamp, but I do remember his alarm clock rattling me awake. I certainly didn't feel as though I'd had a full night's sleep, and it was still pitch dark. In a few seconds Al clicked on his radio, and the familiar theme song of "Tundra Topics" came booming through the dark room, signaling to us it was 9:20 P.M. "Mush! Mush! Mush on you malamutes, wherever you go . . ."

"Tundra Topics" is a radio show, broadcast in Fairbanks, giving messages to people in the Bush from their friends in town. This seemed to be Al's major connection with the outside world. He filled us in with background on most of the people receiving messages. He was wide awake now, and I think we disappointed him with our lack of fresh enthusiasm.

At last the radio was turned off. We went back to sleep and all was quiet until dawn shivered in through the frosty windows. Al got up, lit a fire and put on a fresh pot of coffee. We stayed the entire morning and were really impressed with his knowledge and concern for the land and its future.

Al had been chief of Nenana for a number of years. He recalled his early efforts to initiate the Native Lands Claim, and he was quite concerned with the progress of the settlement. We guessed he was in his mid-70s. He enjoyed part of each year out at his cabin, where he and his wife had raised their children. He still ran a short trap line on snowshoes and did fairly well. Before we left we hauled a few loads of firewood with the dogs. Al seemed to enjoy seeing the dogs work, perhaps remembering days and dogs gone by.

We left with directions for reaching Lake Minchumina. We meandered from lake to lake, wondering which one was the real

Starr Lake named on our topographic map in honor of our new friend. The prevailing north wind had sculptured the lakescape. As we left the lee of the trees the snow was soft and knee-deep. Farther out the ice was swept clear and the going was easy. Three-quarters of the way across, we hit rows of cresting snow waves lapped up by the wind. On the far shore, great dunes drifted hard as rock. As we moved into the next strip of trees the snow softened and the pattern repeated itself.

For the next two days we searched for the notorious Seven Mile Mountain. Both Al Starr and a Fairbanks pilot had told us to use this mountain as a landmark. Time for the Third Law of Dog Sledding: Beware of all directions given by Natives or pilots. Natives know where they are going and pilots can see where they are going.

Any good-sized tussock would have been obvious from the air in that flat country. Our view from the ground was limited by the spindly black spruce muskeg all around us. We couldn't see the mountain for the trees, but that's exactly what made traveling there so interesting. The far horizons were cut off so we became more aware of the close features in our view.

A beaver lodge, disguised as a snowdrift, reminded us of the endless activity below. Many generations of beavers had packed the mud and sticks to make that comfortable dome. I could picture the beaver sunning himself on top of his lodge on the first warm spring days. He'd welcome the geese and watch them swerve and glide to the water. Some mornings a skiff of ice would present a great slippery show. By summer the beaver would know each pair of nesting ducks. He'd ripple his way around the shore, saluting each secret nest with a dive and a slap of his tail, just to make those serious, motionless hens blink.

A study of our map produced a compass reading, and we aimed off toward our unseen goal. Late on the second day, we spied a 50-foot pingo (Eskimo word for conical mound) about a mile ahead.

"You don't suppose that overgrown tussock is Seven Mile Mountain do you?" John asked.

"No, it couldn't be," I answered, "but we better check, just in case."

There, on the far side of the humble hump, a nicely packed trail led off toward our predicted location for Lake Minchumina. Within an hour we were pausing on the shore, surveying the 360° view. To our left opened the wide mouth of the Foraker River. Its source, Mount Foraker, was named Sultana, the Woman or Wife, by the Minchumina Indians, pairing her, the second highest mountain in the Alaska Range, with Mount McKinley, the High One.

The Foraker River was dammed by a sixteen-hundred-foot ridge to the north. The frustrated river just relaxed and spread over the low country, forming the lake beneath the ice before us. Thirty miles of shoreline contained the waiting water, allowing a trickle of a creek to escape. At our backs, miles of spongy muskeg oozed off toward the Kantishna River, under the route we had just meandered.

This meeting of many waters, our landmark, meant we would soon meet our friends, the Bishop family. We aimed for a dark spot on the far shore, expecting a cabin to materialize before we crossed the expanse. As we traveled, five smaller spots appeared, and thereafter we were greeted by the five Bishops.

A grand tour was followed by lots of good visiting and good eating. We asked of the wilderness life and the Bishops asked of town. Our answers were squeezed in between helpings of the Great Feast. Mary Bishop had saved a mountain of moose ribs. With them she served home-grown, homemade sauerkraut. We all celebrated as if we had been on the trail two years rather than just two weeks.

This particular moose was worthy of celebration, not only for its fine taste. During the entire hunting season, both Mary and Dick and their three sons, Dan, Sam and Doug, had hunted faithfully every day. Their winter's meat supply was roaming around out there somewhere, but no Bishop could track it down. On the very last night of the season, Mary heard something stumbling around in her frozen garden. She ventured out under the bright moon, rifle in hand. Her echoing shots called the rest of the fam-

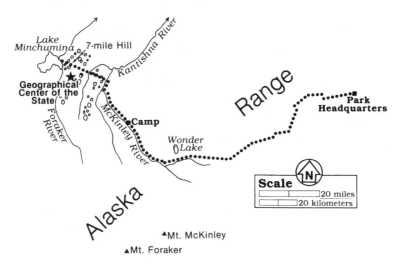

ily. Soon they were busy at the five-hour-long butchering job. With the moonlight and some lanterns, the chore was completed. Procrastination at that point would have produced a nine-hundred-pound moose-cicle! For the next five days we shared the life of this family. Outside, the snowfall continued day and night. John and I made nervous jokes about the deep trail that would be waiting for us. In my journal I noted some impressions of our visit:

February 20
Much to do here and much satisfaction in the doing. The life presents problems, but the answers are at hand. Just takes a little thinking and doing. All these Bishops seem proud of their self-sufficient ways. I admire their GET-UP-AND-GO!

February 21
Dick returns from his trap line with a dead wolf, his first of the year. He's happy, but regrets the timing, considering my feelings about trapping. I can't rationalize killing animals for the sake of high fashion, but I do understand the need for cash to buy kerosene, flour, warm clothes, and the thousand other things a family needs. Trapping is a way to earn some of that money, and live in the Bush at the same time. The whole family has learned a lot about the animals just in watching for signs. These skills were essential in the past to obtain fur for clothing and meat for the table, and should be kept alive along with respect for the lives taken.

February 23
It's darn good that Alaska has room for people to get out and try this kind of life. It's good these lessons are passed on, understood and practiced. What better gift could parents give their children, give themselves, give their fellow man?

Chapter 9
Too Much of a Good Thing

OUR FIVE DAYS of visiting with the Bishops slipped by as quickly as the three feet of fresh snow accumulated on our abandoned sleds. Some winter angel had shaken out her rugs. The frosty dust had carpeted the world below. Every twig and needle bent in a delicate balancing act where the slightest nudge or softest breath destroyed the stability.

I had wished for an early snow when I saw the first star in the August twilight. Again, on my autumn birthday, I had blown out the candles, asking that the snows come soon and deep. Perhaps I had been greedy and now I would have to manage with too much of a good thing.

Dick and Mary planned to accompany us for a few days. As our expanded party headed off across the lake the clouds of McKinley teased us with a brief view, not of the whole mountain but of a white shoulder in the gray clouds. This was enough to give us our bearings as we began the second stretch of our adventure. Four hundred miles of trail remained to reach Ruby and my teaching job.

Traveling with two additional teams felt strange at first, but the adjustment was a cheery one. Our trail-hardened dogs seemed so serious compared to the carefree Bishop bunch. Reaching the end of the broken trail, our light-hearted mood was somewhat subdued. The snow was deeper than we had ever experienced on previous trips. Dick stepped off the trail and sank in up to his thighs, an expression of disbelief on his face.

Out came the snowshoes. John and Dick took turns out in front, but even then the going was extremely slow. Each step required three movements; one to lift the heavy snowshoe, the second to shake off the snow and the third to step forward. The second trail breaker had an easier job, following along and stomping down the leftover islands of deep snow. Next came John's team, hurtling through the soft trail like so many horses in a steeplechase. John's single-file, Canadian harness rig was perfect for this narrow trail. The 20-inch-wide sled tracked well in the 19-inch-wide path.

Following John's team came one of the side-by-side teams. The dogs bumped each other off to either side, but with a fair amount of effort, they could keep up. The third team enjoyed a generous trail. Mary or I rode the runners to weight down the sled, keeping the dogs from overtaking the teams ahead. The last team zoomed along like a herd of thoroughbreds. Not only did we have to weight down that sled, we had to ride the brake.

With such a gradation from beginning to end, we switched the last three teams around to share the work. John's dogs remained in the lead, to take advantage of the single-file harnesses. I wondered if his dogs were proud of their responsibility or begrudged their unfair share of the work?

After gaining only four miles of this slow trail the twilight forced us to make camp. We gathered in the cozy wall tent for dinner, while the fire crackled away in the Yukon stove. We reviewed the day and anticipated the morning's prospects. Sharing the toils of the trail produced a warm camaraderie.

The next morning the Bishops reached their turning point. We munched a little lunch together and said our good-bys. "Let us know when you reach McGrath," Dick said. "We'll be thinking of you and hoping you find good trail long before reaching Telida."

"Oh, don't worry about us," John answered. "This snowshoeing might help us burn off some of that good food we had at your place."

"Thanks for everything," I added. "We'll drop you a note from McGrath."

We controlled our teams as the Bishops turned around and flew off toward Minchumina. We sipped another cup of tea and then continued on our quiet way, minds full of pleasant memories of our visit. I tried to ignore how slow we were going. Even John's long legs had difficulty wading through the deep snow. At dinner that night we marked our camp on the map. We had put in a long day and come only seven miles, an all-time record low for a full day's travel.

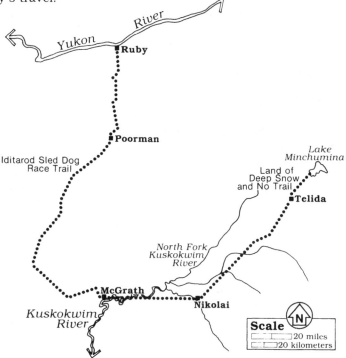

We toasted our Fourth Law of Dog Sledding: Never sit still while the snow is falling; the trail just gets deeper. That night, when I went out to close my sled tarp, I longed for a star that would hear a weather wish, but the low snow clouds intercepted my message.

For the next six days the snow kept falling and our routine was the same. We woke up with the first light and were on the trail by sunrise. Coffee breaks were short and camps were made in the dark. John did the hardest job, breaking trail up in front. I snowshoed behind him, returning to the teams if there was a tangle.

At least the sleds tracked better than in previous years. We didn't need gee poles. My sled had a five-and-a-half-foot basket. John's was a foot and a half longer, allowing extra room to spread out the load, which kept the weight lower. We vowed to build even longer sleds in the future. The runners were "toed-in" by one and a half inches in the front, which kept the sled going down the middle of the trail.

From time to time I relieved John by going in front. Our pace would slow considerably, but John would have a breather and the variety helped break the monotony of the trail. According to our plan, we should have reached Telida four days after leaving Minchumina. The way we were going it would take 14 days!

I began to ration our supplies. We had grown accustomed to a fancy menu, but now our goodies were disappearing. Starting before Christmas, I had baked double batches of cookies, fruit-cakes and banana bread. One batch would be enjoyed immediately, the other would be stored in the great outdoor freezer to be saved for the trip. The Christmas sausages that John's folks sent from Wisconsin were the treasure of the lunch bag. At home I had carefully sliced and divided the greasy meat. With the temperature well below zero we craved the fatty sausage.

With the new rationing program our meals returned to the basics: plain cereal for breakfast and greater proportions of instant mashed potatoes and rice for dinner. Gone were the days of plentiful bacon, cheese and meat. The dogs also received half-portions. We sympathized with their disappointment. I remembered some advice I had read in *Sourdough Sagas*:

On the road to the gold diggings, don't waste an ounce of anything, even if you don't like it. Put it away and it will come in handy when you do like it.

Now, we liked the burnt Logan bread, colored purple by the blueberries which I had purposely packed clear at the bottom of the food box.

On the seventh day we were ready to make another hungry camp. The sky was dark and we were feeling the strain of the slow going. Suddenly John let out a whoop. I was certain he had stepped in a wolf trap. When I caught up with him, he was taking off his snowshoes. He just stood there, watching my expression. When I felt the packed trail under my feet I echoed his whoop. We had hit someone's trap line trail. Below the six inches of new snow there was a solid base. The dogs could go ahead on their own! We raced ahead for another mile and then reluctantly made camp.

The next morning the trail carried us over a forested ridge. On the other side we met an even fresher snow-go trail, which followed the lazy bends of a river, hopefully the Kuskokwim River. A few miles downstream we rounded a wide curve. On the far bank a cozy row of cabins appeared — the promised land of Telida, an Indian village.

A man with a pail in each hand walked toward the water hole in the river, a little dog following at his side. When the man spotted us he dropped both pails, spun around and ran back to the village. The dog scampered past his master, his tail tucked between his legs.

We pulled up the steep bank where the entire village had gathered to meet us. The villagers huddled in small groups, curious yet shy. Several of the young men broke the silence and helped us chain out the dogs. John Dennis, a middle-aged man, invited us to return home with him for a cup of tea.

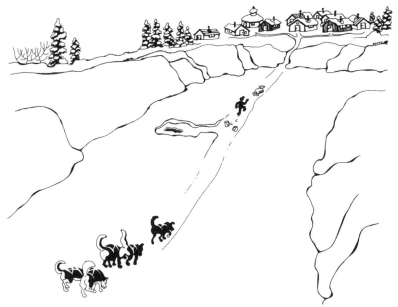

Inside his large one-room cabin the grandmother, wife and five children all found seats, leaving the two chairs at the table for us. On the wall a small portrait of Jesus smiled down. Two bowls of steaming rice appeared and some pilot crackers and jam. Betty Dennis served the hot tea, and we relished the tasty meal, although nobody else seemed hungry. We answered questions and returned smiles to the quiet old and young.

A group of young men came through the entryway. They invited us to spend the night in the community center. They helped us drag our sleds over to the impressive log structure on the edge of town. For a village of five families, this elegant log building was an accomplishment of cooperation they rightfully were proud of.

Soon a generous supply of firewood appeared. The hall served as the school most of the time; now the remains of the classroom were moved to the side, but the education continued long into the night. Small groups filtered through, eager to visit. We learned about Telida; Telida learned about us.

There had not been a dog team in that part of the country for a long time, so we were quite a novelty. Some of the older teenagers could remember the last village teams, but the younger kids had grown up on snow machines.

"We sure like to see your dogs," said a dark-eyed boy. "How much you gotta feed them?"

A girl recalled, "My uncle, he used a dog team to check his line. They never ran out of gas like his snow machine does."

We asked about the village store, planning to buy enough food to get us to McGrath. Our cache of supplies would be waiting in the post office there. We were disappointed to hear there was no store. The mail plane had not landed for three weeks. The entire village was as low on food as we were. I understood why nobody ate with us at the Dennis' home. The treats were strictly for the company.

"You might ask the schoolteachers," a teen-age girl advised. "They always lend us a little extra when we really need it."

We were embarrassed to ask the teachers, but after 10 minutes with them we felt comfortable and explained our problem. They were happy to lend us some tea, macaroni, pilot crackers and margarine. We visited for a while, happy to hear their enthusiastic approach to education. The couple often held classes in their own small cabin when temperatures made the large school a little drafty.

Mrs. Chevalier suggested, "Why don't you ask Steve Eluska to break trail to Nikolai? Nobody's been over the route since Christmas, and we've had a lot of snow since then. There'll be good trail from then on. Steve wants to go to McGrath to see the Iditarod teams come through. Maybe if you paid for his gas, it would help everyone."

We found Steve and presented the idea. He considered it and returned to check with his family at their cabin, 20 miles out of town. The Eluskas were the only family that had brought in enough gas the previous summer. They had hauled it up the Kuskokwim in their river boat.

Steve returned the next day. His folks had agreed to the trip and we planned to leave in the morning. The snow was still coming down.

About noon the next day Steve roared out the trail. For the first day in over two weeks the sky was clearing. Betty Dennis and a few of her kids rode on our sleds as we passed the row of small cabins. Everyone came out to wave good-by and wish us good traveling. At the edge of town our riders hopped off and returned home.

The dogs trotted along with their tails unfurled over their backs like so many flags in a parade. All we needed was a couple of days of good weather, allowing us to follow Steve's trail to Nikolai, a village 50 miles to the west. The trail followed the old mail route used by dog teams before the first mail plane flew into McGrath in 1924. The trail crossed long swamps. If the wind blew, or the snow clouds returned, we would be back on snowshoes. Steve could easily reach Nikolai in a day, but we would take at least two, even on a good trail.

We were crossing one of the long swamps when we sighted something dark ahead. Getting closer, we recognized Steve's snow machine. We feared a breakdown. We hadn't expected to meet Steve until we reached McGrath. As we pulled up Steve relaxed on his padded seat, leaning back against the handlebars. He whistled softly to the dogs, coaxing them near his "iron trailbreaker."

As they passed by he flattered each dog; "Come on by, black dog. You're a good leader, eh? My old machine won't hurt you. Come on by. You've been pulling that team all the way from McKinley, you must be tired. Maybe you should ride up here with me. Maybe I'll sell this and get me some dogs too."

As the team passed, they swayed their hind ends, attempting a friendly wag while confined by their harnesses. They recognized a new friend when they saw one.

"Is there any trouble?" I asked.

"Oh, no," Steve answered. "I just wanted to warn you about the next creek. The moose punched big holes in the trail, and you better be real careful when you come down there. If those dogs are going too fast, they might get an arm stuck in a hole. You wouldn't see the tracks before you came over the bank so I came back to tell you."

"Thanks for the warning, Steve," John said. "It sure is great having your trail. If this weather holds we should meet you in McGrath in five days."

"I'll meet you before then," Steve answered. "I'll camp with you tonight. I've been timing you on my new wrist watch. You're making about seven miles an hour. Not too bad. I'll look for a camp you can reach before dark." With that he set a button on his intricate watch, strapped on his helmet and roared off, leaning his machine in a tight arc to avoid the dogs.

John and I looked at each other. What a mixed-up situation! Here were two Caucasians, traveling by dog team, visiting an Indian village in the middle of the Alaska wilderness. Now our progress was timed by a complicated stopwatch and the trail was made by a high-powered machine.

We enjoyed an interesting evening, comparing camping methods and sharing each other's food. Steve's mom sent the best fried biscuits I had ever tasted, as well as some delicious moose steaks. Combined with our noodles and tea, we all enjoyed a feast. Steve's wonderful sense of humor was delightful. He teased us endlessly, timing everything we did — 45 minutes to break camp and pack the sleds, 10 minutes to harness the dogs . . .

Even though Steve had traveled the trail since childhood, there were places where he had trouble finding the way. Once when his machine got bogged down in deep overflow, we hitched up the dogs and pulled it out. Now we could tease, too.

We neared Nikolai after two days' travel. John and I camped out a few miles from town. Steve spent the night with some friends. Early the next morning Steve returned to check on us. We joined him for coffee at his friend's cabin.

Steve's host was rumored to be the shaman of Telida. A mysterious aura surrounded him. I was reminded of historical accounts I had read of other shamans. In his eyes I sensed a power of dark forests and smoky huts, moonless nights and unexplainable circumstances. I was both intrigued and frightened.

From Nikolai to McGrath the trail was like a freeway. Nearly everyone had gone as far as Petruska's fish camp to see the Iditarod teams. I was anxious to visit there again.

We stopped at the camp in the middle of the afternoon. Most of the race teams had already passed through. The Petruskas had gone all out to take care of the hungry, tired racers. I knew how much the mushers appreciated their hospitality. Under the table was a great selection of freeze-dried concoctions, the best the "Eddie-Bean" catalog offered. These were left in token payment by the mushers, who were grateful for the moose stew, homemade bread and other wholesome treats.

We left before dark, planning to stop for the night at a cabin Steve knew of. Unfortunately the squirrels and marten had moved in during the absence of the owner. Some enterprising trapper, or perhaps the owner himself, had set traps in the windows to discourage the furry visitors. The inside was a mess.

In the light of our last three candles, we cleared a spot for our sleeping bags. The barrel stove was soon crackling, but with the first warmth the roof began to leak. We slept between the drips, or under them, scarcely caring. We celebrated our successful trip with hot tea and the last of the rum, saving one portion to leave on the shelf for the cabin's owner. We were soon asleep, drips pattering down to accent the steady snoring. Outside the dogs accompanied us with a good-night howl.

The next morning, under clear bright skies and -25° temperatures, we headed off toward McGrath. Steve went on at full speed. We pulled in about the middle of the afternoon. Some friendly residents flagged us down and invited us to stay at their place. On the way there, Steve found us and we arranged to meet the next day.

Our friendly residents were missionaries, but we sensed they didn't have too much of a following in McGrath. Something felt wrong about being there and we became increasingly uncomfortable the longer we stayed with them. Perhaps we were contrasting the sincere generosity of Telida with this do-gooder attitude.

We met Steve for lunch and celebrated with a hamburger. The old gut-bomb never tasted so good! We paid Steve for his gas and asked him to return some groceries to the teachers. Steve shared the good news that the plane had landed in Telida as soon as the weather had cleared.

We picked up our supplies at the post office and prepared to leave McGrath. To get to my Ruby teaching job on time, we had to cover two hundred miles in the next four days. John and I vowed the Fifth Law of Dog Sledding: Limit your trip by the amount you can carry on your sled, not by some commitment with a calendar.

Steve had done more for us than break trail to Nikolai. He had guided us through his country with the special care of a good friend. We enjoyed his outlook, his sense of humor and his cheery disposition. Without his help we might have been in serious trouble. The 50 miles of deep snow between Telida and Nikolai could have taken us over a week on snowshoes. Our supplies had barely held out for four days. We were grateful to Steve but, more important, we valued his friendship. We would miss him, and without his stopwatch, would we ever again learn to judge sun time?

We loaded the sleds and took off. Steve drove my team, with me perched on top of the load. A half-mile down the Kuskokwim, we whoaed the dogs and said our final good-bys with warm hugs, hearty handshakes, and many wavings until Steve disappeared over the bank on his way back to McGrath.

Now we steamed along the well-packed Iditarod Trail. A strange contradiction teased me; I enjoyed the advantage of the civilized trail, yet I missed the unmarked country we had traveled through during the past three weeks. Thirty-five race teams, as well as the supporting snow machines, had passed this way the week before. The trail was littered with dog booties, candy wrappers, syringes, batteries, and other flotsam and jetsam justified as part of the Great Competition. We were covering the miles with ease, yet something was lost along the way. The compromise was efficient, but disappointing. I didn't understand how someone could travel through that clean, beautiful country and leave such a disrespectful mess behind.

About midafternoon we caught up with the last two race teams. Their sleds were disconnected and they were in the process of winching their dogs down a steep creek crossing. We had never seen any bank demanding such caution so John went ahead to evaluate the danger. He returned shaking his head, a slight smile on his face. Without any explanation he whistled his dogs ahead. I followed down the bank, passed the roped-up dogs and whizzed around the bend in the creek.

When the teams caught up we stopped for a short visit. I mentioned the littering problem. The racers seemed surprised that a little garbage "way out in the middle of nowhere" could matter. Later that night, we were making camp when they came by. They had thought over my complaint and apologized. They promised to be more considerate in the future.

We pushed the dogs those last four days, covering twice our normal 25-mile average. Finally we climbed the long hill which led down to the Yukon. No gems ever sparkled as brightly as those twinkling lights of Ruby at sunset on March 14. After 30 days on the trail, I would begin teaching the next morning.

Albert and Dolly Yrjana showed us the little house I had arranged to rent. We unpacked the sleds, staked out the dogs, and joined the Yrjanas for a dinner of king salmon, the specialty of the Yukon.

John stayed in Ruby for a few days before heading upriver to return to Fairbanks. We said good-by in the morning before I left for school. I listened for the Ruby dogs to announce John's departure. When the signal was given I moved to the classroom window, just in time to see his team disappear over the riverbank. My own dogs, back at the house, echoed a disheartened refrain. None of us liked being left behind.

Chapter 10
On the Brink of Breakup

.

FOR SIX WEEKS I taught at the Ruby school, with 17 students ranging from kindergarten to the eighth grade. The teaching went smoothly, and I learned along with my students. As the days melted by, my spring fever equaled the kids'. This was my first extended stay in a bush community. I was impressed with the feeling of the past that surrounded the gold mining town. In Fairbanks, and in Alaska in general, the proportion of older people in the population seems to be out of balance. Perhaps many Alaskans retire in warmer climates. In Ruby I had the opportunity to spend time with some real sourdoughs.

The Yrjanas, my landlord and lady, were inspiring examples. Then in their early 60s, they had more enthusiasm for life than many of my contemporaries. Albert, with white hair, rosy cheeks, and twinkling blue eyes, was always ready for a joke. His wonderful Finnish accent made his teasing all the sweeter. He ran a marten trap line, sometimes checking it on his long cross-country skis.

Dolly was a cheery bundle of energy. She giggled about little things like a schoolgirl. Her light-heartedness was treasured by all her friends. Dolly came to Ruby as a young girl, working with her family to run the Fisher roadhouse. Now she was busy getting her seedlings ready for transplanting to the greenhouse or garden at the appropriate time. Her kitchen counters were covered with boxes and trays of germinating seeds. Dolly would add the love and hard work to produce the best fresh salad on the Yukon.

Another amazing Ruby lady was Altona Brown. She was among the first Indian women to come to Ruby, sharing Dolly Yrjana's claim to residency since 1917. Altona was a strong woman, proud of her independent ways. She fished in the summer, hunted in the fall, and trapped in the winter. I loved to visit in her tidy home. A kettle of hot water was always ready for tea. On the walls were sepia-tinted photographs of her relatives and friends. Their expressions held the wisdom and peace of the past.

Altona would tell stories of her life with her husband, the Dago

Kid. They and their children fished at a camp a mile upriver from Ruby. Back in the 1930s, the family dried tons of salmon for their own team and to sell to other mushers. Each winter the Dago Kid would take a sled filled with salmon and a team of new pups over the hills to the south. He'd meet the McKinley Park rangers, sell the entire outfit, and return on snowshoes.

Dog teams were making a comeback in Ruby. The Iditarod was attracting mushers, and Emmitt Peters, Don Honea and Howard Albert, all of Ruby, placed well in the race during various years. Their village was proud of them.

One morning on my way to school I met a snow machine pulling a load of firewood. I recognized one of my students driving the machine. Riding on the back of the sledload of wood, looking proud and wind-blown, was his grandmother. Suddenly I realized what had been bothering me about life in Ruby.

I respected the old and I had hope for the young, but I was disappointed with the people my own age. After meeting older Natives, who were efficient at, and proud of, their subsistence skills, I expected to find the same values in their children. With a few exceptions, drinking and welfare checks seemed to have undermined those independent attitudes. The return to the dog team indicated a reconsideration of the old ways and this was encouraging.

On April 25, my last day of teaching, I was anxious to be free and footloose. The air fare back to Fairbanks would take half my earnings, so I planned to run my dogs back as far as I could go. Breakup was imminent, but to my inexperienced eyes, the Yukon still looked plenty safe. I asked others' advice, but nobody was very encouraging. Even dear Dolly teased me about getting marooned on an ice floe when the Yukon ice let loose.

Ten minutes after dismissing school for the last time I had my sled packed and my dogs harnessed. A few special good-bys to favorite friends and students, and I was over the riverbank on my way to Tanana. I didn't look back until I was a mile out of town.

Those people had been right. The trail was horrible. Both runners sank through the slushy snow. The dogs slogged along, breaking through with each step. I continued on, hobbling awkwardly after my sled.

After several miles of this mistake I pulled over to the riverbank. I guessed the time to be about six o'clock. I lay on my sled for a long time, welcoming each new star as it joined the twilight. I had been wrong about the trail, but I was right about being on my way.

Later that night, maybe eleven or twelve, the bright moon came up. We returned to the trail and were delighted to find the snow frozen by the night's drop in temperature. This set our routine for the next four days — traveling after midnight and on into the next morning as long as the trail held up, and then sleeping during the warm daylight hours. I hadn't been on the long trail alone since the Iditarod, but those fifteen hundred miles gave me confidence and I looked forward to the three hundred miles to come.

In the twilight of the next morning my team suddenly roared ahead, as if chasing something. Expecting to find a moose at the next bend in the river, I was quite surprised to see a flock of spring geese rise from the open water along the shore. The dogs took chase and I tightened my grip on the steering bow, laughing out loud as we zoomed up the Yukon. Goose music and a bird dog for a leader! What next?

I reached Tanana, two hundred miles upstream, after traveling four nights. I met no one along the way. John's old trail was a faint depression in the snow, but it gave a firm bottom under the new accumulation.

I stayed overnight with some friends and departed a little behind schedule the next morning at four o'clock. The sky was just beginning to glow as my sled slipped over the high riverbank down to the icy trail 20 feet below. A chorus went up from the Tanana dogs, starting at the west end of the village and following me to the east. The abrasive sound of my sled skittering on the ice echoed up over the bank, magnified by the cold air. Although we were not seen, many sharp ears followed our progress.

I tried to use the directions given to me in the village. Features seemed to fall in place, but I had a knack for making maps fit wherever I wanted to be. Three miles upriver from town we turned to cross the Yukon. Somehow crossing that great river in width seemed a thousand times more risky than traveling two hundred miles of its length. I directed Cabbage from one bare ice patch to the next. When our zigzagging course reached the south shore, we all were relieved. The first rays of sun were transforming the ice into a sheet of prisms.

Ducks were a common occurrence and I anticipated the chase they would provide. The trail wove along sloughs lined with tall, frosty marsh grass, cattails and tamarack trees. Finally the trail dropped onto a good-sized creek. Fresh overflow water was unavoidable, but the farther I went, the more a queasy, suspicious feeling invaded my mind. At times Cabbage refused to go ahead. When I went up front to investigate, I was horrified to find him perched on a point of ice; deep, brown water flowing around him on all sides. There was no alternative but to go up into the trees.

"Trees" was being polite. The alder thicket was a dog musher's

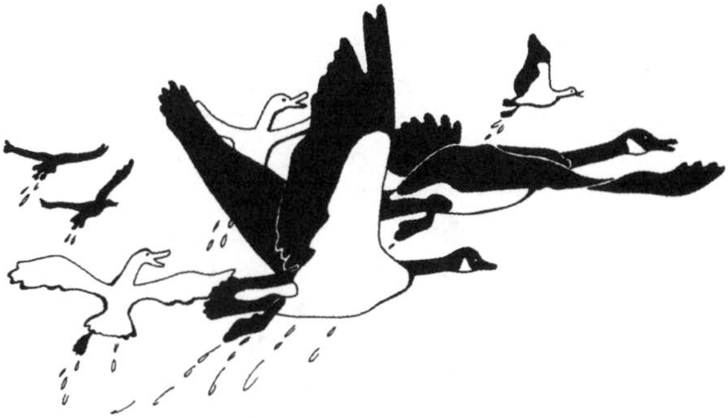

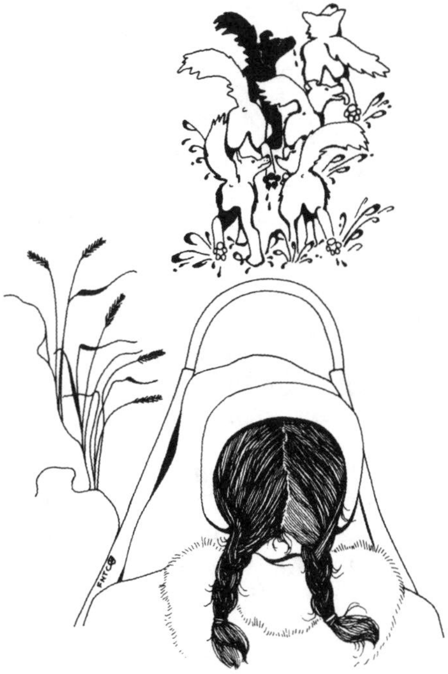

nightmare — four-inch trunks intertwined as they stretched diagonally to the sunlight of the open creek. To maneuver through this maze was a frustrating pain in the neck — and the forehead. As soon as I spotted substantial ice again we left the bank. The ice was strong, but the overflow on top was getting deeper. The basket of the sled was submerged under the current. My choice was to either stay dry on the bank but get nowhere, or get soaked in the channel and make miles. I couldn't afford to be comfortable. I knew the creek couldn't last forever.

After two more nervous miles the trail finally turned up onto the south bank. The dogs roared up the steep pitch with great enthusiasm. First a few sharp curves and then the trail forked abruptly. Both branches were used equally. I didn't have long to decide which way to go for the dogs tugged off to the right. That way looked good to me, so I let them tear along.

In 30 seconds, I discovered the attraction. There in the middle of the trail were the remains of a freshly killed moose. I dragged the dogs past and on down the trail another 10 yards. This was just far enough to see the trail loop back on itself, forming the other half of the fork. The trail was a dead end, not only for the moose, but for me. I sat down on my sled and cried. There was no way I would return on that creek. My bridges hadn't burned behind me; they had just melted into the water as I passed.

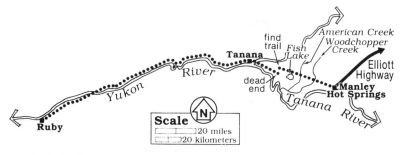

My initial response was panic. I pictured headlines reading: "Breakup strands woman and dog team somewhere between Tanana and Manley." I unfolded my soggy map and tried to figure out where I was.

Slowly my location made sense; the hills were to the north, the river valley to the south. The Fish Lake trail had to be somewhere to the north. I strapped on the snowshoes and broke trail in a straight line to the north. After floundering around for about 10 minutes I gave up. The snow was too wet. Snowshoes can't walk on water.

I lashed the webs back on top of the sled and struck out on foot, punching through to my knees with each step. The dogs sensed the seriousness of the situation and followed behind without commands. The sled plowed a furrow behind them, hanging up on every beaver-chewed stump.

About an hour before sundown we reached the main trail, running at right angles to our own path, just as predicted. There were no fresh tracks, and the sun had melted much of the north side of the trail, but still we were ecstatic at our discovery. We traveled a few more hours to celebrate. When my weariness caught up with me I tied the sled to a tree and unharnessed the dogs, leaving them clipped to their neck lines. I pulled out my sleeping bag and stretched out on the sled, my head resting on the gentle upswing of the front of the basket. The temperature was so mild, I didn't have to snuggle down inside the bag.

Sometime in the middle of the night the late moonlight glazed the trail. I packed up and left to take advantage of the improved trail. Just as dawn was threatening to undo the frosty handiwork my team eased downhill into the Fish Lake drainage. The trail meandered through the tall grass. As we reached the edge of the lake, 10,000 wings pushed down and 5,000 ducks and geese took flight. The dogs were delighted with their surprise. I was thrilled. The sun loomed on the horizon, radiating behind the whirling wings.

My heart was thumping loudly as the dogs picked their way across the lake. The ice appeared safe and solid, except for some open water around the shore. Dark leaves and many bird droppings had melted four or five inches into the ice, leaving a pitted, spotted surface.

On the far side I caught snatches of the trail directing me toward the obvious path up a creek, leading away from the lake. When I reached the creek I found it flowing wide open. Again I bushwhacked through the forest, aiming toward the possible trail. The snow had melted in large patches, so my only hope was to find a cut through the forest.

After an hour's search I was back on line. The panic of being lost was less intense this time. I was just getting mad at wasting so much precious time looking for the trail. I was cutting the season short and there was a chance of being stranded in that never-never time of breakup. For a week or two, traveling cross-country was nearly impossible; the snow was too soft, the ice too rotten and the rivers too swift and cold.

Reaching American Creek, I realized just how close I was cutting it. Icy water filled the creek bed from bank to bank. Thank heaven for Labradors! I told myself. Cabbage bellyflopped in and I nudged the sled into the wheel dogs, who were desperately trying to think of an alternative plan. The current swept the sled downstream, but the creek was only eight feet wide, and as soon as the first three dogs got good footing on the other side they pulled the rest of us out. I couldn't touch bottom, so I just hung on to the steering bow and flutterkicked.

Safe on the other side, I rummaged through my sled bag for some dry clothes. The dogs shook wet halos in the sun. Thanks to my stuff bags and the big sled tarp, my gear stayed fairly dry. I teased the dogs, "That wasn't so bad, ye land lovers. Let's head on to Woodchopper Creek and take a real swim!"

Now I traveled day and night, resting only when I could go no farther. Time was critical and the night temperatures weren't cold enough to improve the trail. The little snow left was too soft for me to ride the runners, so I just walked up with the 'dogs. Except for my overnight in Tanana, I hadn't seen anyone for six days. I talked to the dogs, and I could understand their responses. They were tired of dragging the sled over the tussocks, yet with a single encouraging word they would pick up their pace and flap their tails. I appreciated their good company.

To be walking over those high, rolling hills felt wonderful in spite of fatigue. This wasn't winter dog sledding but it was a chance to see the seasons change. The smells of spring were in the air. A flock of excited sandhill cranes whirled by, trumpeting their joy to the rising updraft on which they rode. Male ptarmigan staked out territories, cackling their advertisements from the tops of the few scattered spruce. The golden grasses of autumn past swayed in the wind and I shared a favorite John Haines poem with my companions:

To Turn Back

The grass people bow
their heads before the wind.

How would it be
to stand among them, bending
our heads like that . . . ?

Yes . . . and no . . . perhaps . . .
lifting our dusty faces
as if we were waiting for
the rain . . . ?

The grass people stand
all year, patient and obedient —

to be among them
is to have only simple
and friendly thoughts,

and not be afraid.

Dropping into Woodchopper Creek valley I could see and hear lots of water. Overflow spread one hundred feet beyond either bank. I took off my dry clothes and packed them carefully in my sled tarp. I went ahead of the dogs to investigate the extent of the water. For the first hundred feet, the water ran about knee-deep, but this was still on top of solid ice. Then I came to the main channel.

The current looked swift and perhaps 20 feet wide. The bank on the far side was overgrown with a dense stand of willows, except at the clearing where the established trail crossed the creek. If the sled got swept downstream and the dogs tried to climb out in the willows, they would never be able to stretch out enough to tug the heavy load up the bank. Clearly I had to find another, safer crossing.

At that very instant something (a moose? a bear?) cracked a branch on the other side. The dogs heard the snap and were eager to chase. I decided to take advantage of their enthusiasm and worry about the stimulus when, and if, I reached the other side. Away they went . . . *ker splash!* The current hit the sled broadside, swirling it to a 90° angle from the dogs. Cabbage seemed to understand the importance of coming out at the clearing, and he chugged up into the current. The sled floated just under the surface, and again I helped the only way I could — flutterkicking.

The far bank held the deepest water and the dogs had trouble crawling up over the edge. Another branch cracked, providing the incentive they needed. Up popped the dogs, up popped the sled and up popped the bedraggled musher, hanging on for dear life. The dogs took off, splashing down the trail, leaving a wake behind the sled.

My dogs have always done a silly thing when they chased something. They know they go fastest on the packed trail. They get so excited, they insist on running full speed, straight ahead, no matter that the tantalizing creature is sitting in the bushes, 10 feet off the side of the trail. I never saw what snapped those branches, but I was content to leave it behind. After about a quarter of a mile, the dogs gave up and stopped.

I hunted for my clothes. There I was, standing naked, dripping wet and shivering. The humor of the situation was just under my frozen smile. Then, with no warning, the most respected, most dreaded wild Alaskan predator entered the scene. A bloodthirsty mosquito attacked my arm. That was that! The season was officially over! I dressed and we hightailed it into Manley as fast as we could go. Unfortunately that wasn't any faster than we were going, but we tried harder.

Thirteen miles out of Manley we hit the plowed road leading to the Tofty mine. I stopped and visited with the Newbaurers, owners of the mine, and enjoyed a hot lunch with them. Mr. Newbaurer apologized for the plowed, gravelly road ahead, and gave us a ride in his big, flat-bed truck. Two miles behind the mine a wide creek icing blocked the road. I thanked him for his help, and convinced my dogs their free ride was over. A few more miles of gravel offered no serious problems. Our progress was slow, but the evening sun was pink on the hills, radiating an energy that made me feel I could go on forever.

Several miles later, on the opposite side of another icy creek, a pickup truck was turning around. The dogs were crazed by the headlights and chased after the truck. Surprise of surprises, the truck was waiting to give us a lift into Manley. Mary Newbaurer had sent word with a bush pilot who had stopped to visit after I had left. Some friends of my friends had driven out and waited for me. Bobbie and Steve helped me load my confused dogs into the truck and we coasted downhill 10 gravelly miles into Manley.

After a long soak in the hot springs pool and a sweet, uninterrupted sleep on my sled, with the dogs stretched out around me in the leaves, I awoke the next morning to the song of a robin, celebrating in the branches overhead. Happy May Day!

I called John in Fairbanks. He borrowed a car and trailer and set out to meet me. The next morning, Bobbie and Steve trucked us out the Elliott Highway to a roaring stream that closed the road. Steve, prepared in his hip boots, helped me get my dogs across. A tall, warm hug waited on the other side. We waved and bellowed good-bys back across the water as Steve returned. Then we piled the dogs into the trailer.

I glowed with the pleasure of being with John again. He repeated all the news of the past seven weeks. I interrupted him unmercifully to ask neglected details, forgotten in his letters.

"Yes, I mushed all the way to Nenana," reported John. "And guess who I ran into there? Al Starr! He was back in town for breakup. We went to the movies together . . . saw The Sourdough and it was great! And on my way into Tanana six snow machines stopped to ask me if that was Morgan up in front of my team, Old 20-mile-an-hour-Morgan!"

On and on, the new ideas flooded my mind. Through the car window I watched the miles slip by. In one hour we covered more country than I could travel with the dogs in an entire day. Yet I had been aware of each drainage I crossed, every river bend I rounded. When I crested each divide I felt a personal sense of achievement. My going was a slow one, but the experience was intimate.

As we peaked over the last summit before reaching Fairbanks, there was McKinley, one hundred miles off in the southwest, a good neighbor welcoming us home. Both our faces relaxed in smiles, understanding that our trail had come full circle. Winter swung round behind us. We rolled downhill into spring.

Chapter 11
Sledding Into the Country

OUR TABLE WAS COVERED with topographic maps in February 1977. The Fairbanks quadrangle was in the center, surrounded by Tanana, Livengood, Beaver, Circle, Eagle, Tok, Delta Junction, Mount Hayes, Black Rapids and Mount McKinley. The creased edges were held together with tape. The paper was soft from use and misuse, folding and unfolding, snow, rain, river silt and squashed mosquitoes. Penciled lines progressed from dot to dot. Scenes of past trails and camps materialized.

I was surprised that the maps covering country north and east of Fairbanks were still clean light green, free from our intruding lines. Therefore I was not surprised, three weeks later, to be on our way to Chicken, Alaska, a small mining community 250 miles east of Fairbanks. From there we would go on to meet friends in Dawson and help that town celebrate an anniversary.

The organization seemed to be getting easier each year. An old battered notebook held "The Lists" from the previous four years' trips. I tried to reorganize them into one complete list:

The List
Kit

Sled repair:
wire, nuts and bolts, cord
pliers, screwdriver, wrench,
repair links for chains
(cold-shuts)

Harness repair:
webbing patches, thread,
needles, snaps, tugs,
neck lines, J's leather kit

Sewing:
safety pins, needles, thread,
patches

First Aid (People):
gauze, Band-Aids, tape,
antiseptic cream, aspirins,
pain killers, cold pills,
eye drops, first-aid book

First Aid (Dogs):
booties, pain killers

Caboodle

books
maps
flashlight

snowshoes
sled tarp
camera, lens, film

Camp

tent, stove jack
stove, pipe, damper
poles
space blanket
ponchos
caribou pads
sleeping bags

blue foam pads
cook kit: pots, lids, cups
  plates, spoons, forks,
  spatula, tea strainer,
  pot holder, sponge
candles: 3 per day
toilet tissue
matches

Clothing

To wear:
wool union suit
two pair wool socks
wool shirt
wool pants
wool sweater
cotton parka
wool mitts
moose-hide over-mitts
wool hat
shoe pacs
To pack in sled:
extra pants

underwear
socks
extra felt liners
insoles
lightweight sweater
insulated shoepacs
To pack in sled bag:
emergency gear
long wool scarf
cuffs
wind pants and parka
extra mittens
extra gloves

Sled bag

stake-out chain
rough lock chain
whip
ice creepers
extra snaps, tugs, neck lines

sun glasses, case
lunch bag
two vacuum bottles
sunburn cream

Magic bag

hair brush
toothbrush, paste
little mirror
soap

washcloth
vitamins
notebook, pen
money

Food

Breakfast:
cereal
brown sugar
powdered milk
bacon
coffee
margarine
orange drink powder
pancake mix
hash browns
Lunch:
sausage
cheese
dried salmon
Logan bread
gorp
instant soup
bouillon
tea
cocoa
instant coffee
cookies

fruitcake
pilot crackers
Dinner:
salmon [cooked, frozen)
ham (cubed)
meat
cheese
brown rice
egg noodles
macaroni
instant mashed potatoes
onions (sliced, frozen)
beans
chow mein noodles
sour cream mix
salt and pepper
soy sauce
margarine
Extras
shortening
popcorn
booze

The old notebook also held favorite recipes and suggestions from the trail:

Logan Bread

1 pound margarine (melt)
½ cup molasses
1 cup brown sugar
½ cup honey
½ cup powdered milk
6 eggs

3 tsp. baking powder
2 tsp. salt
2 cups raisins
2 cups nuts or seeds
lots of berries

3 cups whole-wheat flour, or enough to form a thick dough

Mix well, spread to ½-inch thickness on cookie sheet, and bake slowly in warm oven. Cut and store in cloth bag. (Use whatever you have around the house, but add no liquid. The margarine and berry juice will be plenty.)

Pancake Mix

1 cup whole-wheat flour
1 cup white flour
2 tsp. baking powder
1 tsp. salt
¼ cup powdered milk
2 tbs. shortening
(1 cup sesame seeds, or ground sunflower seeds)
(¼ cup bran)
(leftover hash browns are excellent
     mixed in pancakes before frying)

Mix dry ingredients and cut in shortening. For 6 pancakes, add ½ cup water to 1 cup mix.

Suggestions:

1. Slice meat and cheese before trip. Spread it out to freeze and then package the individual pieces in one bag.
2. Paint tent roof with flame and water retardant. Prevents spark holes and drips. Air out well before using.
3. Bring a small can and lid for saving extra bacon grease from breakfast. Some grease is good in the hot cereal on cold mornings.
4. Snow-seal boots well, before trip.
5. Pick a strong food box. Handle holes make lugging to the tent easier.
6. Look for good buys on candles and fruitcakes after Christmas.
7. Canned sardines are nice for a special lunch. Must thaw them out inside your shirt all morning.
8. Fill vacuum bottles with hot water to make a variety of instant drinks throughout the day.
9. Bright calico pockets sewn in tent are handy and cheery.
10. Tea strainer, without handle, takes care of spruce needles in snow water.

Although organization was easier, it was half past five the evening of March 12 before the truck was finally packed, and we still had several last-minute stops in town. By seven the low-riding pickup finally rolled south on the Richardson Highway. The sagging springs were due to a dozen sled dogs, curled up in their hay-filled dog boxes on top of the bed of the pickup; two heavily loaded freight sleds, lashed on top of the dog box; and two tall, heavy mushers folded up in the front seat.

The pickup was thanks to fellow mushers, John Bryant and Peggy Kuropat. They were starting the same trip, but leaving from the other end, Eagle Summit, one hundred miles north of Fairbanks on the Steese Highway. They would come up the bank of the Fortymile River in about a month. At the highway bridge near Chicken, their pickup would be rested and waiting.

We planned to meet John and Peggy in Dawson, Yukon Territory, Canada, where we all would join the celebration of that city's 75th anniversary of incorporation. Several other teams would fly to Eagle and carry the official celebration mail up the Yukon, some 80 miles to Dawson. John and Peggy planned to travel with these teams from Eagle.

After a five-hour drive to Tok, we appreciated the warm little guest cabin offered by Bill Arpino, a 1973 Iditarod musher. When we arrived after midnight, the welcoming lights were still on. I had written to Bill asking for information about the route to the Yukon.

Over a yummy sourdough breakfast the next morning, Bill filled us in, while his wife filled us out. By midmorning the low-riding pickup and passengers were on their way out the Taylor Highway.

Reaching Chicken, a winter-quiet mining community in the Fortymile country, we learned more about the trail. The next morning we cleaned out the truck, loaded up the sleds, and dropped over the bank of the South Fork of the Fortymile River. The base of an old trail held the dogs. In the sifting, snowy, gray day, my eyes could not decipher the trail so I left the navigating up to Cabbage.

The Fortymile was gold mining country and the remains of old cabins along the banks reminded us of the past. Friendly ghosts of old prospectors sat under the trees and watched our parade. Their dreams of fortunes found and lost were not important any more. Their lives on the river were what really had mattered in the end.

The trail our lead dogs followed was set by those ghosts and their lead dogs. Sleds heavier than ours had brought in supplies to last the entire winter, not merely a few weeks. The campsites we picked probably had been canvas wall tents before. The smell

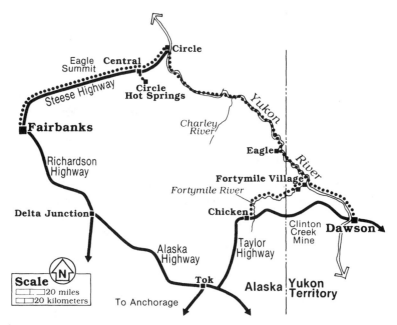

of spruce smoke had enticed curious whiskey jacks before. The sudden chorus of our sled dogs was only an echo resounding from the bluffs of time.

Four days later we reached the mouth of the Fortymile River. A long row of cabins was all that remained of the abandoned 1888 mining supply camp of Fortymile. We found one weathered cabin that looked heatable and scrounged some dead cottonwood with the aid of the flashlight.

The morning dawned clear and cold. We squinted out across the dazzling river, searching for fresh tracks. The Yukon was only a quarter of a mile wide there, so we suspected the main channel must be farther out. The traveled trail would probably be out there.

Some French Canadians, fresh from Montreal, stopped in for coffee. They had spent the night partying in another cabin at the far end of the village. They worked at the asbestos mine at Clinton Creek, a few miles upstream on the Fortymile. They were eager to be making big money, although they could feel the asbestos fibers in their lungs after only three weeks' work. The trade-off was worthwhile to them. Their accents reminded me that somewhere in the last 50 miles, the river, hillsides, and even the very snow, had been claimed by England. We were now in Canada, but the Northland looked just the same to us. The Queen of Winter reigned here, and she was the ultimate power.

About a mile upstream the south channel braided back into the main river. We aimed diagonally for the northern shore hoping to pick up a trail somewhere. Skirting along the shelf ice under the sheer two-hundred-foot-high bluffs, a packed snow-go trail pleasantly surprised us.

"Well, those dog teams must have made good time," said John. "I don't see any paw prints or even a brake mark. The snow machine tracks have covered their trail and they have been here several days, I'd guess. We'll never catch them now, but we'll have a good trail into Dawson."

March 17 (journal entry)

Twenty miles downstream from Dawson. Today the snow swirled into our faces all day. In the middle of the afternoon a snow bunting came zooming along in the wind, singing its heart out. It circled over our sleds two times, just a few feet over our heads. Then it disappeared into the snow downriver. This is a full month earlier than we've ever seen snow buntings before. Omen of early breakup?

Several miles below Dawson the river made an exaggerated bend to the south. Around the corner the entire width of the river was covered with a jumble of ice blocks. The labyrinth of ice looked as if the river had changed its mind after freezeup. The bergs, blocks and plates of ice were heaved up in jagged angles, some only 3 or 4 feet high, others 10 to 12 feet above the rough surface. The dogs wove their way through the frozen floes, following the snow machine tracks.

About three-fourths of the way across the tracks showed a hole, freshly frozen over with dark ice. The snow machine had gone through, but somehow it had managed to get out and continue on the other side. The dogs trotted on oblivious to the danger. I gripped my steering bow and held my breath as the sled slipped over the smooth ice. Our weight was stretched out for 20 feet, from Cabbage's nose to the tail end of the sled runners. This was much safer than all the weight of the snow machine resting on its six-foot length. Reaching the south bank, I felt extremely comforted by the willows that marked dry land under the snow.

When Dawson appeared on the northern bank we hit a fresh trail that crossed the river again and took us up off the ice. How many teams before us — Natives, prospectors, trappers and mail carriers — had shared the same relief getting off the ice and pulling into Dawson?

A row of well-seasoned log cabins stretched along the riverbank. Children appeared out of the snow piles along the road. They confused us with the mail teams, who we learned were still en route.

Truckers on the road from the Clinton Creek mine reported their progress and predicted their arrival the next day. We made camp in the deserted campground on the south side of the Yukon. "We're probably the only tourists to have this whole campground to ourselves," John joked. "Yeah, it pays to travel in the off-season!" I responded. We walked back across the river, getting a good view of the city. The streets etched tidy blocks on the level plateau overlooking the river, cutting back to the base of the mountains, perhaps a quarter of a mile. On one of these back streets we found the cabin where Robert Service had lived. On my first trip north in 1965 I had visited the historical site. During the summer visitors can take a peek inside.

The weekend's festivities were in full swing. Beauty queen contestants, bedecked in bright parkas of heavy blanket felt, paraded around on snow machine floats. Each beautiful parka was decorated with various appliques of contrasting felt and fur trim in the Canadian tradition. The customary beauty pageant satin sash was also draped over the parkas.

Over on the snowy ball field a game of snowshoe baseball was in progress. We admired the players' agility and speed on the long snowshoes.

A Smoosh Race was advertised for two o'clock. Smoosh, a Dawson original, exemplified the spirit of the winter gathering. Two teams of six members each gathered at the starting line. Getting into the smoosh was half the contest. Roughly speaking, smoosh are 10-foot-long skis, with bindings for six smooshers.

I use the term *skis* freely, as the two by fours certainly did look like skis, but in fact they didn't slide at all. A coordinated effort by the team was needed to step forward. "Right, left, right left," until one member tottered a bit, started to giggle, and then the whole team fell apart. Laughter erupted. The six smooshers were falling, catching each other, trying to regain balance, but their attempts were hopeless. Some of the contestants had primed themselves with a little beer, which didn't help the balancing act. Spectators laughed as hard as the contestants. We loved Dawson and her cheery people.

"This must be like back in the gold rush," I commented to John as we walked back to feed the dogs.

"Yes, this town has a refreshing spirit. Everyone seems to know each other, and they're all glad to get together and whoop it up!"

On Saturday morning the entire town gathered on the plowed ice-bridge crossing on the Yukon. Two hundred people, bundled up against the -20° weather, waited for the highlight of the weekend. I could hear the stirring music of a marching band coming down the long hill from Clinton Creek. A real marching band, right here in Yukon Territory! I felt that exciting "waiting-for-the-parade-to-come" tingle.

The music rapidly grew louder. I pictured the marchers jogging down the steep hill, never missing a note. How did the tuba player ever keep up? How did he keep his lips from freezing? My anticipatory smile drooped a bit when the bright-red city of Dawson truck rolled into view, loudspeakers blaring away on top of the cab. The "marching band" rode in the front seat, looking all too much like a tape recorder.

My smile beamed again when behind the royal escort came the five beautiful dog teams, prancing and dancing with the excitement. Old-timers remembered and the children dreamed. The mushers coaxed their dogs past the crowds, checking their language as their dogs took full advantage of the pats and compliments.

After the teams were comfortably bedded down, the mushers pulled up chairs around a big table in the hotel's bar. Rounds of beer appeared, and the tales of the trail bubbled up. In Eagle the volunteer trail breakers, whose snow machine tracks we also had followed, had urged the dog treams to travel the safer route along the road. Their close call in the jumbled ice below Dawson had prompted the caution. Appropriately, the mushers had taken their advice, although the truck traffic along the road was also a considerable threat.

We described the river conditions. Everyone raised their glasses toasting the noble sled dogs. "A good dog team can get through where snow machines fear to go."

A gala steak dinner was on schedule for Saturday evening. Most of the town attended; all the mushers were invited as guests of the city. The meal was great. The waltzing, rocking and rolling, and polkaing that continued late into the night were even greater.

The next morning Dawson's mayor offered his home shower to all the mushers before they headed back. We all took advantage of the generous offer. While waiting my turn I read a poem by the mayor's wife, Sue Carrel. She had written it while away at school in the south. She allowed me to copy it in my journal, and I have treasured it ever since.

If I were north
and it were now,
the sky would be
a brighter blue.

The snow would sparkle,
cling, and melt
and spring would
be a breath
of yet to come.

But I am here.
The sun is warm,
the crocus blooms
and spring is here
too soon.

It wants the flavor
of having to wait
for one more snow
to anticipate
the now of beauty,
the now of spring,
the time to hear
the sparrow sing.

I am here
in the sun today,
but all my soul wants
to be away
to the land
still blue and white.

After everyone was clean we said good-by. The three mail teams were flown back to Fairbanks on a chartered plane, courtesy of Dawson. John and Peggy wanted to stick around town for a few more days but we were anxious to hit the trail downriver. We hoped to mush all the way back to Fairbanks, some five hundred miles. The date was March 23. The temperature had dropped to -30°, but the snow bunting's warning predicted an early breakup.

A visit to the Dawson General Store provided a five-pound loaf of Heidelberg rye bread. A visit to the post office on Monday morning provided the cache of supplies we had mailed ahead. The sleds were lashed and the rye bread packed safely in a protected spot of honor. We glided out the trail waving farewell to the spirited little town that had won our hearts.

The trip downriver went smoothly and easily, almost uneventfully, except that each morning we sawed off slices of rye bread to toast on the stove. The swede saw worked well on the frozen loaf and the camp robbers enjoyed the crumbs. Our old trail had set up like concrete in the cold temperatures. We made excellent time, averaging about 40 miles a day, past the Fortymile River, and on past the United States-Canada border. An actual cleared line through the forest shot down the hills on the north bank of the river and ricocheted up the other side. The land was claimed by different governments, but the Yukon River was bigger than boundaries could hold. The ice that was now Canadian would flow into the U.S. come breakup.

In Eagle, Alaska (where John McPhee "came into the country"), we stayed for a few days. My neighbors from "down the tracks" of my Chulitna days had moved to Eagle. We had great fun remembering that winter on the railroad. The way friends keep bumping into each other in this gigantic state can only be explained by two words, "that's Alaska."

Continuing down the Yukon we found pretty good trail, thanks to the people who lived along the river. Every 50 miles or so a trail led off to a cabin in the woods. We visited many of these river people. They were not close to each other in distance, but the winters on the river made them very close in friendship.

Their lifestyle made a deep impression on us. They were living a basic subsistence life, earning an adequate income from their trapping to supply themselves for the next winter. Most were young couples with energy and enthusiasm to make a comfortable home in the wilderness. They valued the life they chose and were more than satisfied to go without the luxuries of town. The time, space and necessity of running their own lives were more important than the security of an eight to five job.

Most trappers along the Yukon used three or four dogs to run their lines. Every musher we met shook his head at our wide, 21-inch basket sleds. They all preferred narrow, 10- to 16-inch-wide, 10-foot-long toboggans, adapted to their narrow, long and winding trails. Keeping two hundred miles of trail brushed out was an enormous job, so the narrower the trail, the better. They also favored the toboggan for breaking trail after a deep snow or in the drifting conditions typical on the Yukon. The only disadvantage they complained of was going through overflow, where the entire surface of the toboggan got iced up and required cleaning. Canvas sides were permanently sewed into many of the toboggans. With the high sides they could carry a considerable load.

The dogs were fed dried king salmon, put up the summer before. Some of the dogs looked heavy and others were mostly bones, reflecting the success or effort of the previous fishing season. During the summer most of the dogs had a long vacation. Their owners would switch to 19-foot aluminum canoes, powered with 7½ or 10 horsepower motors.

When the river was low, exposing a good beach, dog power was an alternative for some people. A pair of strong dogs could pull a canoe and passenger upriver. One dog would be hitched to a bow line and his partner would follow, tugging on a stern line. The ride back downriver would be compliments of the mighty Yukon.

For several nights in a row we accepted warm invitations to overnight with people along the river. These comfortable nights were enjoyable; we exchanged stories and learned about life on the river.

When we reached the mouth of the Charley River it was time to camp again. After supper, as I filled the vacuum bottles for morning, I commented to John, "It's almost a little boring to travel on such a big river with such an easy trail."

John blew out the candle and warned, "Um-hum, but don't say that too loudly. We're not home yet."

But my words were out. The next morning the Winter Queen's response was roaring on the other side of our canvas wall. Several inches of snow had piled up overnight, but the trail was still visible. We took our time with the last cups of coffee. The dogs were not anxious to go out into the wind, but they uncurled and came to their places along the towline.

Once we were out on the river we felt the full force of the storm. The wind blew low over the snow, picking it up and scattering it anew. The ground storm, combined with the falling snow, brought visibility down to about two feet. Black Cabbage, at the head of my team, was out of sight. So much for my "boring" conditions on the river, I guiltily told myself.

Progress was very slow that day. When a puff of smoke swirled by the dogs' noses, and then ours, we all perked up. The dogs chased down the smoke and pulled into a sheltered creek bed. To be out of the blowing snow felt wonderful. We followed the trail as it wiggled around the bends of the little creek.

Suddenly we climbed a steep bluff and were in the front yard of a beautiful, old, two-story cabin. The snow was drifted around the windows, allowing only about a foot of glass to show. Out behind the cabin a few sled dogs announced our arrival. The lady of the house came to the door and invited us in. She was a bit startled by our sudden appearance. She called her children down from upstairs and introduced them to us. Her husband was in Fairbanks getting supplies.

Coffee grew into dinner and dinner grew into overnight. With the wind howling outside, we were easily persuaded to stay and visit. Ingrid Ruckles, a Swede, and her irresistible children, were refreshing company.

The next morning dawned clear and still. The trail leading off the bluff was scoured clear of drifting snow by the night's wind. After good-bys, John led out the trail, with my eager chasers lunging at the lines to follow. At the bottom of the bluff we not only caught up, but piled up into John's team. The trail down on the river was completely drifted in. The dogs couldn't even feel the base under the snow.

On came the snowshoes and the old familiar procession of breaking trail. As I tromped along, I worded the Sixth Law of Dog Sledding: Never complain about conditions being too easy . . . at least not out loud.

Four very long days later we reached Circle City. We entered the quiet cafe and asked for two coffees. The steaming cups appeared and a frozen pizza was popped into the oven for us. Then we learned that the cafe was not officially open. Both the coffee and the pizza were compliments of the proprietors, Frank and Mary Warren.

They radioed Pat Oakes, 30 miles down the Steese Highway, announcing we had arrived and were on our way. Pat had our next cache of supplies stored in her guest cabin and she radioed back, encouraging us on. We clocked ourselves along the road, using the mileposts. The road was packed hard, and there was little traffic. Eight miles an hour was our steady speed, on the straightaway or over the hills.

In Central we stayed with Pat, who had been my principal-teacher in Ruby. She filled us in with news from that village and from all over the state as well.

A side trip to Circle Hot Springs was a most refreshing treat. The Olympic-size pool, filled with 100° water, was ready and waiting. We had the entire pool to ourselves. After a few minutes every sore snowshoeing muscle relaxed and gave up the fight. Circle Hot Springs was another old gold mining community. As we floated around on our backs in the wonderful water, we again remembered the mushers who, no doubt, had relaxed in the same hot springs so many years before.

Our race with the snow bunting's warning was stepped up the next day. We followed the road toward Eagle Summit, the 3,600-foot high point on the road back to Fairbanks. Nearing the top we met the mechanical harbingers of spring, the road crew. The grader scraped the road down to gravel, but, luckily for us a tiny strip of snow remained, allowing the sleds to slip along.

Closer to the summit, 10-foot drifts had turned the crew back toward Central. We left the road right of way and headed up for the summit. Rocks poked out where winter winds had whistled, but the dogs picked their way around them. The view from the top showed a much easier route on the south side, following a low pass connecting two small creeks.

"That must have been where the early mushers put their trail," concluded John as we stopped on top to look for a way down. "The slope's much gentler and there might even be good ice. That's the place for a dog team, but not a road."

We angled down toward the road on the north side. After a breath-taking trip down, we settled in, following the contoured path of the road again. With the good wind pack we were back down below the tree line just in time to make camp.

The next day, April 8, we met the road crew coming from the Fairbanks end of the road. As they scraped down to gravel a new accumulation of snow fluttered down behind them, giving us just enough to squeak by on.

On April 10, Easter Sunday, we turned onto our home trail overlooking Goldstream Valley northwest of Fairbanks. The dogs recognized the familiar route, a favorite weekend run, and trotted along with their tails high and a new lilt in their pace.

We stopped for lunch at a sunny clearing on top of the ridge. No longer would this be just our Sunday trail. Now we knew it reached to Dawson; it reached to the people along the Yukon; it reached to the ghost mushers of the past — trappers, miners, mail carriers or just plain adventurers like ourselves. They had blazed the trail and they had been with us on our journey.

Chapter 12
Trail to Heaven

OUR YEARS WERE ESTABLISHING a satisfying rhythm: working for wages in the summer, hunting and fishing in the fall, living more at the cabin in the winter and traveling with the dogs in the spring. To afford the necessities of this life we willingly gave up the luxuries once valued. Living at our own pace, close to the seasons, brought great satisfaction. Chopping open the water hole in the creek and carrying home the icy pails of fresh spring water was more worthwhile than the ease of turning a faucet.

"Going out to eat" meant homemade bread and peanut butter under the old spruce, not steak dinners at a fancy restaurant. We spent our time doing subsistence chores and learning to improve our skills. The doing gave as much pleasure as the results of the doing. Stretching our combined earnings to carry us through the year was a challenge. Society classified us in the poverty range but we considered ourselves very wealthy. Depending on ourselves, grateful for healthy bodies, eager spirits and a bountiful land, we were slowly building a sense of security.

Because I was employed only part of the year, a large proportion of my salary was withheld in taxes. Each year, some of that money was refunded; we relied on it to buy supplies for our spring trip.

In March 1978 I was making hopeful pilgrimages to the post office each day. On March 3, heads turned when my "yahooooooo!" echoed through the little College, Alaska, post office. The beautiful brown envelope, with my computer-typed name showing in the cellophane window, sat in the mailbox. Plan A for the afternoon immediately went into effect: first stop, the bank; second stop, the Alaska Feed Company; third stop, the grocery store.

That night John's carpentry shop floor was a map subdivided into four "counties" — Denali, Paxson, Delta and Salcha. A mountain of supplies and dog food materialized in each county. The next morning the mountains were boxed and on their way to the post office, to begin spring trips of their own.

Our friends, Ron and Ruth Hurlburt, were caretaking a lodge

on the Denali Highway, a summer road connecting Cantwell and Paxson. In their Christmas card the Hurlburts had offered to drive us (all 14 of us) to the lodge for a starting point of our trip. (The road had been kept open those 65 miles for the Army Corps of Engineers who were studying a proposed dam on the Susitna River.) We planned to go across the Denali Highway, go down the Delta River, maybe up Black Rapids Glacier, up the Goodpaster River, over to the upper Salcha River and back down to the Richardson Highway.

Ron arrived in town the same day as the tax refund came. Two days later, when he finished his business, we all drove out the Denali Highway. We stayed with the Hurlburts for a few days as we organized to hit the trail.

An old December snow machine trail unraveled like a ribbon down the highway to the east. The valley, 30 miles wide, was bound by mountains on both sides. A leftover white Christmas ribbon tied together stretches of windblown gravel, which appeared and disappeared between deep drifts wherever the road curved against the dominant direction of the wind. Only this hard-packed ribbon resisted the ever-changing snow pack. That Christmas angels had traveled by snow machine — an absurd image — but surely this was their trail, still waiting for us like an unexpected gift.

We scurried downwind, with its helpful nudge at our backs. The dogs were eager after three days of loafing, so we made good time. Awed by the far horizons, we neglected to make camp in the last stand of timber, which we whizzed by in the middle of the afternoon. In the twilight, we stopped for a quick hot cocoa from the vacuum bottle and a study of the map.

"We better keep going till we reach Little Clearwater Creek," John said. "It's only about four more miles. The map shows green there, so we should have firewood and shelter from the wind."

"It's so good to be on the trail, and it's so beautiful with the stars popping out," I answered. "I could just keep going all night."

The view coasting downhill into the creek valley was a little disappointing. The only timber was a narrow band of willow and alder, thickly edging the creek. "Where there's a willow, there's a way," I quoted a pun-loving friend of ours. We turned the dogs off the trail. All the snow that had been swept off the road in the previous 30 miles seemed to have landed in the Little Clearwater valley.

My first step off the sled runners never touched bottom. Out came the snowshoes, and the clumsy routine of making camp on the "big feet" slowly came back. An hour and a half later, the dogs were chained out and fed, the tent was up, our gear was

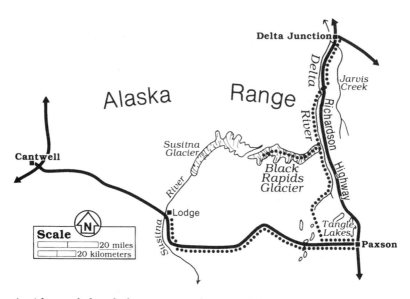

inside, and the sled tarps were battened down against the dark
winds. I filled the pots and vacuum bottles with water from an
open hole in the creek. John sawed a huge pile of dead wood and
stacked it outside the tent.

Dinner was more than fashionably late, but the liver, onions
and rice gave a wholesome satisfaction. The golden glow of the
candlelight in the white canvas tent emphasized the warmth in
my heart, happy to be back in our snug little tent home. As I was
drifting off to sleep a wolf howled somewhere in the hills. The dogs
replied with their own chorus and I snuggled down next to John,
thankful for the wilderness lullaby.

The next morning reveille was sounded by the water ouzel out
on the creek. I stuffed dry twigs into the stove, added some bigger
sticks, and struck the match on the metal stove top. The
reassuring crackling spread in the stove and I returned to my
cocoon. Five minutes later, the temperature was comfortable
enough to venture out.

The treeless horizon glistened a pale pink with the first low
light. The air was peacefully still, the temperature -10°. The cold
felt clean and sharp.

Three days later we reached Paxson Lodge at the junction of
the Denali and Richardson highways. Our supplies had been
mailed to the lodge the week before. We celebrated with hamburgers and coffee at a table by the window. After eating we
tracked down the manager and inquired about our supplies.

"Oh, so you're Mary Shields," he chuckled. "I was wondering

when you'd show up. I just finished packing all your stuff into that shed over there. Mail just got here about an hour ago. Pretty good timing — the mail only comes once a week, you know." No, as a matter of fact, we didn't know. Must have been those angels again.

Retracing our trail back out the Denali Highway, we traveled by moonlight. We stayed in a small cabin near the trail and continued toward Tangle Lakes in the morning. Turning north off the road, we raced along where we pleased, the wind-packed snow supporting the dogs. Following the deserted road had been great, but following the lay of the land was even better.

We stopped for a coffee break near Fourteenmile Lake, in an amphitheater of snowy mountains. Our plan was to follow the flow of the lake to its outlet, which eventually would take us to the drainage of the Delta River. We sat on the sled, marveling at the 360° view of mountains.

My eye caught a narrow gap on the high horizon, leading exactly where we wanted to go. "Look, John," I suggested, "why not take that shortcut up and over, instead of going the long way around?"

"It's a very intriguing little notch,"John admitted, "but it'll be a real climb getting up there." He studied it thoughtfully and then said, "Why not? Let's give it a try!"

Climbing one thousand feet in less than a quarter of a mile was a scramble, but the greatest challenge came from the frozen springs oozing out over the slope. That ice, combined with the boulders jutting up, made certain we would not retreat by the same route, even if conditions looked bad on the other side.

Resting in the rocky outcroppings near the top, we were scolded by a well-hidden ground squirrel. We were as surprised to hear him as he must have been to hear us. We selected a small lichen-covered rock to take home for our collection and then pushed on to the summit.

At four thousand feet we reached the pass and stepped over into the winter's accumulation of drifted snow. On the steep descent the dogs broke trail, but farther down on the plateau I went ahead on snowshoes. The valley of the young Delta River stretched before us, making our shortcut a success. By noon the next day, we were navigating around the open channels of the Delta. Farther downstream we enjoyed perfect ice conditions, carrying us 40 miles in a few easy hours.

In a wonderful little camp under the branches of some robust river bottom spruce, we could look back upstream and see our silhouetted shortcut. In another day's easy travel we reached Black Rapids Glacier and camped in an old moraine undulating with 10-foot-high drifts blown in off the glacier. We dug out a flat spot for the tent. The dogs burrowed in like bears denning for the winter. The next day Larry Mayo and Dennis Trabant, glaciologists for the U.S. Geological Survey, arrived from Fairbanks. The pair had been studying Black Rapids Glacier for 10 years and had come to make their biennial survey of its movements and changes in size. In February they had invited us to join them, if the timing worked out. We felt privileged to go up on the glacier with these experts and were eager to learn from them. Dennis and Larry traveled on double-tracked snow machines. (Our lead dogs groaned happy little moans when they realized they would be following the iron trail breakers).

The morning of our ascent the glacier was hidden by a whiteout, a snowstorm of white on white where visibility was diminished to two feet. Larry and Dennis knew the moraine so well, they could navigate by familiar boulder patches and ridges as they came to them. Following their trail we were perfectly safe, even though we had no depth perception. The heavy machines pulled sleds carrying supplies and fuel, leaving a foot-deep trough behind them. The temperature was about 25°, making the snow soft. We could only ride the runners, as running behind or even kicking was useless with no bottom in the trail. Our sleds were fairly light, carrying only three to four days of supplies and firewood.

By midafternoon the whiteout quickly turned into a dark-out. Suddenly a tent appeared in front of us. The figures of Larry and Dennis materialized like dark ghosts.

"We can't find the old route in this poor light. Hard to tell up from down now, so it's time to make camp," Dennis said. "Want some help staking out the dogs?"

"No thanks, Dennis," John answered. "We're going to sink our tent poles to hold the stake-out chains."

"Good," said Larry, "I'll get to work on this kerosene stove. After you get set up come on over for some dinner."

As we unpacked the sleds I thought I heard someone yell. Larry and Dennis appeared to be busy getting their camp set up, so I was puzzled. Our dogs were all looking beyond the tent, ears pricked up as if they also heard something. When I heard the sound again, I looked up and there came a skier, dwarfed by his gigantic pack. He glided down to the tent, obviously very happy to meet us. He exploded into jubilant words.

"Boy, am I ever glad to see your camp. My three partners and I have been on Mount Hayes for the past 30 days. We almost made the summit, but bad weather turned us back. We're trying to get out to the road, but with this whiteout it's awfully slow going. I've been scouting out a safe route through the crevassed fields. My partners are following me; they're each pulling a sled."

"Well, our fresh trail should get you out to the road in four or five hours," Larry said.

"That's the best news I've heard in a long time! I gotta go back and tell my buddies. O.K. if I leave this heavy pack here?" He disappeared back into the snowy night.

In half an hour the whole party arrived in camp. We shared hot drinks, but they were restless to get going before the snow covered the trail. As they hoisted their 80-pound bundles, Larry offered to haul their gear down with the snow machine.

"I could bring up our extra fuel cache," he offered, "and you guys could enjoy the ski down."

A chorus of "Yaahooos!" went up as the skiers loaded their gear, including their empty five-gallon white-gas cans — bulky items to dangle from a pack — onto Larry's sled. The elated skiers pushed off, flapping their arms like birds, free of the weight that had been part of them for over a month. Their singing, yodeling and shrieking disappeared into the thick snow down the glacier.

When Larry returned later that night we all gathered in the roomy mountain tent and shared dinner. The kerosene heater purred away and took the chill out of the air.

"Welcome to Black Rapids Glacier," Larry said.

"To Black Rapids!" we all answered.

"Fantastic," exclaimed Dennis.

"Fantastic!" we all echoed and crunched on the fresh celery provided by Dennis.

"Hey," I wondered, "how did you ever get fresh celery up here?"

"Easy," replied Larry, "in the lager box."

"What's a lager box?"

"See this Coleman cooler? See these poly-bottles full of hot water? Well, the hot water is the heat source and the cooler is the insulation. We heat up the water every night and keep all our fresh food from freezing. The weather can get pretty grim up here, and we have to be out in it to get our work done. Coming back to the tent and enjoying a really good meal means a lot. We're convinced it's worth the trouble."

"I'm convinced, too," I said. "Let's toast the lager box with another celery."

As we did, something clicked, and Beethoven's Ninth Symphony crescendoed in.

"And you thought we roughed it up here, didn't you," Dennis commented. His FM radio was picking up the University of

Alaska's station, more than a hundred miles away in Fairbanks. "Must be bouncing off the mountains just for us," Larry explained.

The weather had not improved by morning. The two snow machines took off into the storm. By early afternoon we caught up. Dennis and Larry already had their camp made. The trail, only a few hours old, was nearly filled in with new snow. Their machines, parked near the tent, were disappearing under five inches of new accumulation. The temperature was soaring to the low 30s, making the snow very wet.

We pitched our tent, but as soon as the fire was going the warm ceiling began to leak. We had painted the panel of canvas around the stove jack with water proofing and spark retardant. The rest of the ceiling was saturated by the snow melting on top. We stretched a metallic space blanket over one side, and safety-pinned plastic bags on the other side. It was only three in the afternoon, but we were all glad to be in our tents for the night. This was no weather to be traveling in on a glacier.

By the next morning 14 inches of snow had joined the glacier. We stayed in the tents most of the day while the storm continued. This was our third day on the glacier and we had planned to be back to the road on the fourth. Our supplies were getting low. Just before lunch, Larry and Dennis came over to our tent. They squeezed in and had a cup of coffee.

"Can you stretch your supplies to last a little longer?" Larry asked. "When you travel on a glacier, you have to take the glacier's terms. I think you'll be really glad you stayed if the weather ever clears."

"I've got to go back out to the truck to get an antenna we forgot," Dennis said. "I could pick up some of your dog food from your cache and drag up some more firewood, too."

"That would be wonderful," John agreed. "We would like to go all the way up. But how will you ever find your way back to camp?"

"I won't be able to see the trail, but I'll still feel it when I go off," Dennis answered. "I'll get going right away, so if it clears off we can make a run for the top in the morning."

The rest of us spent the day in our tents. Larry had lots of paperwork to catch up on. We finished our book, read the map — every word of it — studied the first-aid book, and then started reading the cereal box.

By late afternoon the clouds had thinned out in places. John and I snowshoed up a side glacier feeding into Black Rapids. When we turned back we had a clear view of camp. For half an hour, we could see across the main glacier, which was over two miles wide at this point. Rugged mountains flanked the other side. We began to get a feeling for just how big it really was. Our camp was just a tiny cluster of specks on the near edge of the great ice river. Going up on that glacier, imagining the slow grinding, oozing and squeezing beneath us, was like going back in geological time. The past dwarfed man's evolution just as the width of the glacier dwarfed our camp. The clouds closed in again and our hike back to the tent was shared by two very humble, very insignificant, very quiet souls.

John had scratched his cornea during the trip, making the brightness of the glacier very painful to him. His antibiotic ointment was not helping much, so the rest time in the tent was good for him. Dennis returned several hours later. We were grateful for the new stock of dog food and firewood.

During the night I was out on one of my regular watering trips. A surprising wind was roaring down the glacier. I accomplished my mission as quickly as possible. Suddenly I realized I could see the mountains in the moonlight. The clouds had blown away. The nippy wind chased me back into the tent. As I snuggled down into my sleeping bag I whispered to John, "It's windy and clear out there!"

"Uhuummmmm," John moaned, not really waking up.

I was so excited I could hardly fall to sleep. I wanted to go back out and look some more, but I knew the dogs would start barking if I stayed out long. I closed my eyes and tried to remember the incredible view I had seen.

From my journal the following day,

Sunday, March 19

Larry and Dennis take off up glacier early. The sky has cleared. We follow with empty sleds. Trail soft and slow going. They find one of their stakes and survey back to two known points on the mountains, bench marks they had put in by helicopter. The distances between the three points tell how far the stake has moved since last fall's survey. They also measure the depth of the snow pack. It's one thousand feet deep! Now I understand why Dennis says Fantastic! so often. It's the only appropriate word.

The temperature is close to +30°, but with the wind chill factor, it feels more like -20°. I marvel they can use their bare hands in fine tuning the theodolite. The air is so clear I can see minute details in the rock faces of the mountains along the glacier. I find my eyes following routes up ridges, along crests and to the summits of the mountains. It really looks possible.

After they're done at one point, they move up-glacier to

*the next stake. We follow, steadily climbing the great ice
river. After the last stake they make a run for the very top
of the glacier, which turns 90° to the south. When we catch
up, Larry and Dennis are circling around and around,
trying to gain enough speed to climb a very steep pitch.
The altitude and fresh snow are bogging down the
machines.*

*John straps on snowshoes and goes ahead. I can tell by
his pace that the altitude is slowing him down. The dogs
don't seem to be affected. I step off my runners and nearly
sink out of sight. D. and L. head back to camp, letting us
enjoy the top of the world by ourselves. The fresh cornice
along the ridge to our north curls over, reflecting an alpine
glow in the sunset. Everywhere around us — miles and
miles and miles of snow and mountains. This is the
highest we have ever been with our dog teams.*

*We both realize we are freezing. Time to go back down.
John went ahead. We just floated down . . . down . . .
down . . . mile after mile. My feet got cold, so I hopped into
my sled, stretched out and relaxed, and sang to my dogs.
By the time I spied the faint lights back at camp, I was
really cold and had to peddle to warm up.*

*I was relieved to smell the cottonwood smoke from our
stove. That meant John was home and the tent would be
warm. John helped me unharness. My hands couldn't do
it alone. A quick, hot dinner and we hit the bags. It seemed
as though we had visited another world, very far away.*

To our disappointment, the snow clouds moved back during
the night. "We better get back off the glacier before the weather
traps us up here again," John warned.

His eye pained him, even sealed under a thick patch and glacier
goggles. He pulled his parka ruff tightly around his face, blocking
out as much light as possible. We thanked Larry and Dennis and
headed down-glacier into another snowstorm. I felt like the blind
leading the blind. One last glimpse back up the glacier; the sun
was streaming through holes in the clouds, making our tracks
look like a trail to heaven.

That night we made camp in the first grove of trees we came
to. Those scrawny, wind-snarled cottonwoods seemed like a comfortable, friendly shelter. Somehow we belonged in the trees.

We talked it over while waiting for dinner to cook. We had been
visitors on the glacier. We didn't really belong up there, but it
had been wonderful to experience that world for a few days. We
were privileged to live on the eternal snows, but we had been

dependent on Dennis and Larry. They taught us to take the glacier on its own terms, to forget our earthly schedule and patiently wait until the glacier allowed us to move. Maybe that's the way it is with heaven.

Chapter 13
Have Dog Team, Will Travel

MOUNTAIN PASSES and glacier crevasses presented fair risks we were willing to take, but the U.S. Military Reservation on the lower Delta River, littered with countless unexploded shells from years of war games, was unfair. We detoured over to Jarvis Creek, a glorious mountain stream flowing down from Mount Silvertip. Following the stream, we zagged back into Delta Junction, where we picked up our cache of supplies and a fresh start with a hot shower at the park.

John's eye had healed enough so his dark glasses were enough protection from the sun, and we headed up the Goodpaster River, aiming for Indian Creek where we hoped to cross over the mountains into the Salcha drainage and a hot springs there. On March 25 the first flock of spring snow buntings looked down upon us, wondering at our tracks. So did the pilot of a small plane.

Charlie Boyd, the pilot, glided over us to land on the river. This was his country, claimed by many years of trapping there. John asked him how the trapping was going.

"Not much fur left in this country any more," Charlie answered. "Oh, there's a few cats down in the lowlands, but every one I take this year will cost me five more next year. I used to live out here, ran a dog team, too. But the land can't take it any more, too much impact. Now I just fly in from Delta, check my traps and go back. It's better this way."

We explained our route and asked Charlie if he'd ever been up Indian Creek.

"No, not very far. But that's the way the Salcha Indians used to come when they traveled to Healy Lake. You'll make it all right. Well, I gotta get flying while there's still light. Enjoy yourselves!" he hollered as he swung up into the cramped cockpit. The little plane soared off toward Delta.

The next day, as we fought our way up the brushy lower stretches of Indian Creek, we remembered Charlie's encouraging information. The weather was playing tricks on us. The temperature on the sled thermometer had floated up above freezing. By afternoon on March 28 it had geysered up to 50° above. Off came the wind parka, the wool sweater, the wool shirt. The buttons of our wool union suits were set loose, and finally the tops were pulled off, with the long sleeves tied around our waists.

Snowshoeing uphill, in deep, wet snow in these temperatures, was extremely uncomfortable. We were soaked to our knees. Even the leather uppers of our summer-weight shoepacs were saturated. The trees thinned out as we gained altitude. From a clearing we saw that Indian Creek's other fork looked less steep. Any Indians who survived the trip had probably taken that other route. But we had worked too hard to gain the 2,500-foot elevation and were too stubborn to give it up now.

About three o'clock we were side-hilling around an especially steep pitch, angling up at about 60°. An unbelievably vigorous spruce rose 30 feet above the hillside. Under the branches, a 10-foot-wide circle around the trunk was snow free. I flopped down in the warm, inviting, dry grass.

John snowshoed ahead to search for a better path up the rest of the slope. He returned half an hour later and reported, "We better make camp here for the night. It only gets steeper ahead. We don't want to get caught on top in the dark."

"That's fine with me," I answered. "This is a wonderful spot to stay. We could spend the whole spring here. I knew you wouldn't pass up this spot."

John confessed, "I figured we'd stop here. I just wanted to look ahead and make sure we can really get over the top this way. If you think the last two miles have been steep, wait until tomorrow. It's really going to be a grunt, but I think we can do it."

We staked out the dogs and made camp. To produce a level spot for sleeping, we gathered up a few spruce boughs from each of the surrounding trees. With these we built a platform four feet deep on the downhill side, the sweetest smelling mattress in the forest.

The sleeping bags were fluffed out on top of the boughs. The wide branches of the spruce above were all the tent we needed. The temperature was holding about 32° at sunset. The tent stove was set up for easy cooking. Our wet clothes hung in the branches over the stove. Finally we stretched out on our wonderful bough balcony, comfortably sleeping with our heads out of the sleeping bags. The moon came out somewhere below us, and the entire mountainside shimmered with an incredible light. Maybe we were just that much closer to the moon.

The sun followed in the moon's path a few hours later; first pale pink, then blushing rose, and finally the softer golden glow which eased out to a clear, quiet morning. We indulged in an elegant breakfast of whole-wheat pancakes with brown sugar

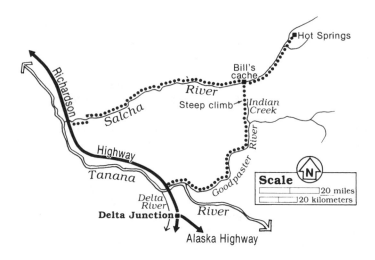

drizzled on top while they cooked in the frying pan. After we had enjoyed the first pot of coffee, we splurged with a second pot, savoring the aroma and cradling the warm enamel cups in our hands. The dogs were sprawled out in the snow, enjoying the peaceful morning as much as we did. Being dry felt so comfortable, we procrastinated as long as we could. By late morning, we agreed it was time to depart.

The next thousand feet of elevation came in less than a mile. Bare-chested John snowshoed a route up a pitch so steep that for long stretches he was bent over, using his hands to balance himself.

The air was calm and warm, about 40°. The view below us was so intriguing, we ignored getting wet. My layers of sweaters and mittens were piled on top of my load. One over-mitt fell off and started sliding down the slope. Too slow to catch the mitt, I had to go down after it. John held Cabbage's collar so he wouldn't follow me. I sat down and wiggled toward the mitten. The wiggle was a little more momentum than I needed and I glissaded down the slope.

"Dig in! Dig in!" John shouted, but I dropped a hundred feet before managing to stop myself. Crawling back up felt like several thousand feet. From then on, I was extremely cautious guiding my team, realizing that if the sled flipped over, the whole outfit would be dragged down.

Three hours after breaking camp we were on top of the pass. Patches of alpine tundra were blown free of snow. We selected a dry picnic table. The dogs crowded onto other mossy islands and stretched out comfortably. Looking back, we could follow the

Indian Creek valley to its confluence with the Goodpaster. Over 60 miles to the south, Isabella Pass could be seen where the Delta River squeezed through a narrow opening in the Alaska Range. Dark threatening storm clouds were developing over the mountains. We pictured Dennis and Larry snowbound in their tent again on Black Rapids Glacier. The wind blowing from that direction was starting to pick up around us, and the sweat we had raised climbing up the last pitch was freezing, quickly chilling us out of our picnic. We couldn't see the route down the north side, but if what went up went down we were in for some tricky sledding.

We double-checked everything on the sleds to be sure all was lashed securely. I eased over the crest and started down first. My dogs chased more than John's did and I was safer out in front, where I had more control. The slope appeared gentler than we had expected. Most of the rock outcroppings were buried in the wind pack.

I gave Cabbage the command to go straight ahead, warning him, "Easy now, easy, Cabbage." He tried to relax the pace but my sled, even with the brake digging in, was gaining momentum. A wake of snow sprayed up behind me, frosting my pant legs. Suddenly the slope dropped out from under the dogs. I was overtaking the wheel dogs, who were galloping along at full speed ahead. The towline caught up and the sled flipped over, dragging the dogs around behind it. Several seconds later we came to an abrupt stop.

A little dizzy, I righted the sled and screamed at the dogs to straighten out. I knew they were tangled, but I wanted to get them moving again, so when John's team came hurdling over the rim above me, we would be out of his way.

"Careful of the drop-off!" I hollered over my shoulder, just as Morgan, John's leader, leaped off into thin air. John repeated the act I had just performed. From my viewpoint the loop-the-loop was quite dramatic. When I saw John stand up, shake off, and swear at his dogs, I was relieved that he had come through safely.

Farther down, on more level conditions, we inventoried for damages: dogs O.K., sleds O.K., people O.K. — only the momentary discombobulation.

I presented the Seventh Law of Dog Sledding: If you leap before you look, be sure to look at the next guy, so you can see what your leap looked like. John agreed, but claimed he wanted to go down first the next time.

In another hour we descended what had taken three days to gain. The safety of the deep snow was a letdown compared to the thrills of the upper freedom, but then we came onto a fresh, single-file wolf trail. The route meandered a bit, but it was interesting to follow and it surely beat snowshoeing.

The map directed us up and over another low saddle which dropped into a drainage that flowed directly down to the Salcha River. We turned off the wolf trail and out came the snowshoes. Even going down the other side, John had to break trail. We combined both teams, attaching my sled behind John's with a crisscross of ropes which kept it following in place. I rode the brake of the second sled, but because the dogs were bounding so slowly in the soft snow, and the pitch was so steep, the sled frequently ran into the wheel dogs.

When we reached the creek bottom, I gave a loud "Yahoooo!" to signal John we had made it. My signal also startled a flock of ptarmigan which exploded out of the willows in front of the dogs. The 12-dog team took chase and I held on for a breath-taking ride across the overflow ice. A thick clump of willows ended the chase, and John and I separated the teams. We rough-locked the sleds with a short chain wrapped around a runner, and with that extra control eased down the icy creek.

A half a mile downstream we learned why the creek was named Boulder Creek. Our tracks looked like a trail through an egg carton. By twilight we were exhausted. We pulled up on the bank and made camp.

From Delta we had phoned Bill Lentsch, a friend who would fly in our last cache of supplies. Bill was not home, so we left a message with a neighbor. We estimated our arrival on the Salcha River to be March 31. We were less than five miles away on the night of March 29, so we figured we had plenty of time to get there.

We slept late the next morning, and were just beginning a relaxed breakfast around nine o'clock when a small plane came droning up the Salcha River. A little later the plane swooped down out of the hills, following our tracks, and circled the tent. The forest was too thick for us to signal back. Bill must have seen the smoke swirling up through the treetops. We threw the camp into the sleds and started down Boulder Creek.

The dogs were forced to break trail, as we were busy clearing the logjams that blocked the channel at every bend. The alders and willows that lined the creek were impenetrable, so we stayed with the creek. I was concerned that Bill would be waiting for us, but John was sure he would just off-load our supplies and return to Fairbanks.

An hour and a half later John needed refueling. We stopped for some lunch, but I was anxious to keep moving. Fifteen minutes later we bushwhacked our way out of the thicket and escaped onto the river ice.

There was Bill's plane. We raced up to find Bill napping on a fallen spruce tree. In good humor he complained he was starving after waiting all morning. When John confessed that we had stopped for lunch, Bill exploded. I quickly dug out the lunch bag. (Bill and John work together as carpenters, and this was their familiar way of ribbing each other.)

"What are you complaining about? You're a day early yourself," John pointed out.

"What do you mean? Your message said March 30, and that's today," Bill retorted. Somehow our message had gotten mixed up.

Bill filled us in on the news. After a month on the trail, we really enjoyed the short visit until Bill decided it was time to return home. He warmed up the engine of his plane and skimmed off over the river "mosquito fashion." We turned the dogs upstream, found our supplies, made camp and reorganized.

On March 31 we left half of our supplies in an abandoned cache, built on standing trees, about 12 feet off the ground. We would pick up this food for our return trip down the Salcha.

The weather had turned cold again. Above the bluffs on the eastern shore two bald eagles circled on the updrafts. Had they wintered there, we wondered, or were they early migrants? In the afternoon a dark object appeared on the river ahead of us. When we were close enough to recognize the wolverine it also recognized us and galloped off into the woods. The dogs burst forward, bellowing and scrambling like a pack of bloodhounds. In their eagerness, of course, they flew right on by where the wolverine had turned off, but we urged them on and enjoyed the ride.

On April 3 the morning coffee was just about to boil over, so I rescued it with the pot grabber, a little clamp affair that came with the cook kit. In my haste, I didn't secure the clamp tightly enough and the pot of hot water spilled on my leg. John tore open the tent door and I flew out into the snow. The cold numbed the pain, and for the next half-hour we piled snow on the red blotches on my ankle and lower leg.

We started another pot of coffee. By the time the snow water had come to a boil and the grounds had been added, gigantic blisters had erupted on my leg. I cut open my long underwear so it would stretch over the gauze bandages we applied on the blisters. I switched to my loose-fitting winter shoepacs, which just barely fit over my fat ankle.

We packed up and took off over another treeless ridge. Our goal, a hidden hot springs, was tantalizingly close.

By twilight we had still not reached our destination. Cabbage was picking the trail down another boulder-strewn creek when he stopped and refused to go ahead. No encouragement or command could drive him a step forward. John stomped past impatiently insulting my black dog. Two steps beyond John went into open water up to his knees. We pulled up onto the bank and made camp. We were close enough to the hot springs to see steam rising from the open water ahead.

We played around at the hot springs for several days, rerouting the main channel, mucking out the thick algae blooms and damming up alternative routes. Many wiggly crustaceans lived in the warm water, which explained the abundant bird life in the area. The springs was in a narrow valley where direct sunlight made it over the ridge for only a few hours a day.

We selected two pools for our bathtubs. Neither pool was quite large enough to stretch out in, but I could curl up and fit and John could settle in with his legs sticking out from the knees down. We planned our bath for the sunniest time of the day, clearing the channel so the hottest water flowed directly into our tubs. We scraped off the thick calcium deposits which covered the rocky surface, and overnight the rocks warmed up considerably. Where the main springs burbled up we could hardly keep our hands in the water, which meant the temperature was around 119°. By the time it had flowed down to the pools the water was a little cooler, but still hotter than a normal bath.

A mountain breeze blustered down the valley, so undressing was undertaken carefully; first the boots, socks and lower layers of clothing. Instantly we lowered our bodies into the water to get out of the cold wind. The air temperature was about 10° below zero. After the top layers were removed we oozed down underwater and relaxed. The water was perfectly clear and our white bodies looked out of place in that exotic setting. The tubs were about two feet deep, and the steaming water flowed through continually. My blisters burst, but I rationalized that the hot water would sterilize them. (They healed up fine.)

We relaxed in the tubs long after the sun had disappeared behind the ridge. When we finally got out, the dressing was completed in the exact reverse of the undressing, only quicker. When our hands got cold, all we had to do was stick them back underwater. I wrapped my freshly washed hair in a towel and made a dash for the tent.

Soon the fire was roaring, and dinner was on the stove. This was the turning point of our trip. We were squeaky clean, rested and ready to return toward home. Our five-week journey had covered some of Alaska's most spectacular country. We respected this "farness." We felt comfortable and at home in the wilderness. Our dog teams had allowed us to travel where no other transportation could follow.

The long April days gave us 16 hours of sunlight. In a week, we backtracked two hundred miles to the mouth of the Salcha. Over coffee that last morning of our trip, we agreed to sell one of the sleds so we could buy supplies to spend the spring out at the cabin. Our wealth was our wandering.

Chapter 14
Dog Trails North

THE LURE of steamy hot springs waiting in the frosty wilderness fascinated us. For the next three years our dog sled trips searched out secret springs. I think their waters were charmed. They gave us the energy to make our dreams come true.

In 1980 we made our big move out to the cabin. During the previous seven years we had enjoyed part of each month out there but when we returned that September we stayed for good. The cabin was home.

John continued his woodworking in a small workshop we built next to the cabin. He used the native woods of the area: white spruce, birch, aspen, alder and willow. A portable chain-saw mill made ripping rough lumber efficient, but the rest of the work was done with hand tools. Several times during the winter John packed up his finished items (dovetailed boxes, small cabinets, furniture and other items) and sledded them into a Fairbanks art shop where they were sold.

I worked on my writing and enjoyed the routine of our quiet life. We both returned to Goldstream Valley, near Fairbanks, to work during the summer.

In 1982, 10 years after John had traveled to the Brooks Range on his first dog trip, we returned there together. John was curious to refresh his memories and I wanted to see it for myself. Winter was waiting north of the Arctic Circle. So were ideal dog-sledding conditions.

As of mid-March, only a foot of snow had accumulated around Wiseman, a community of 13 loyal residents on the middle fork of the Koyukuk River. Old-timers there couldn't remember a winter of so little snow. Most of the creeks and rivers in the area were high with overflow ice. Without the thick insulating layer of snow this would be expected. All that ice was as good as, if not better, than a packed trail for dog sledding.

Leaving Wiseman we zoomed up the road to Nolan Creek on "bunny-power." Snowshoe hares darted across the trail every few minutes and the dogs raced wildly along, forgetting the heavy sleds they pulled.

The hares had been at a high in their 10-year cycle for the past four years. Their heavy browsing had pruned the willows, alders and even some of the spruce. Traditional hare theory has them crashing every 10 years, with a slowly growing population bringing them back up to a high. I guess the hares around Wiseman weren't traditional.

"From my view behind you today," John commented at camp that night, "it looked like you had a white, loose leader. I've never seen so many rabbits!"

The next day we were traveling up the north fork of the Koyukuk River on bare ice. A pair of ravens played with me and my dogs chased their shadows. I made up endless songs to sing to my dogs:

> When it's springtime in Alaska,
> I'll be on the trail,
> Mushing up the Koyukuk,
> If you pay my bail.
> The sled dogs are a-yapping,
> And the ravens twirl and croak,
> Mushing up the Koyukuk,
> Even if I'm broke. . . .

As we slipped north an easy 40 to 50 miles a day, John remembered the slow days of snowshoeing the same stretch back in 1972. What had taken him nearly two weeks to cover that year we now skimmed over in three days.

In front of us we could see the river narrowing where it passed between two dramatic mountains. Our USGS map called them Frigid Crags on the west and Boreal Mountain on the east. Robert Marshall, young explorer of this region, named the mountains back in 1929.

We stopped for lunch between the two quiet guardians, turning our backs on the north wind and letting the sun warm our frosty faces. The morning temperatures were stubbornly holding to 30° below, but by noon the thermometer read from 0° to +10°. We lunched on smoked salmon, Logan bread and thick strips of frozen cheese, which we thawed in cups of hot bouillon. We savored this special lunch stop. We were picnicking on the threshhold of the Gates of the Arctic, the two mountain peaks Frigid Crags and Boreal Mountain.

The Arctic — I used the term freely for years. Now, with some experience in the boreal forest, which lay to the south, I could really appreciate the differences and the more severe demands the environment put on plants and animals that attempted to live there.

And the Arctic was not going to allow us to pass without some effort. The afternoon after we passed through the Gates of the Arctic, the blue sky faded a bit and a haze gathered in the south. When we pitched the tent that night a light sifting of snow sprinkled down on the canvas. By the next morning eight inches had fallen.

As we turned off the north fork, following Ernie Creek which led to Anaktuvuk Pass, a divide in the Brooks Range, the snow was still piling up, now a foot and a half deep. The south wind, a chinook chasing up from the Alaska Range, brought temperatures close to freezing. The wet snow was heavy on our snowshoes, and our mileage for that long day was only seven miles.

We made camp in a stand of willows. The northern limit of spruce was left down on the lower stretches of Ernie Creek. The back third of our sleds held dry spruce, which we planned to save for our camps in Anaktuvuk. I gathered dead willow from the surrounding grove, sometimes having to dig down quite a way to find a piece long enough to haul back to the tent. The new snow was now two to three feet deep, on top of impressive wind-packed drifts. Three days earlier we could have skipped up the pass on that wind pack and been to Anaktuvuk Pass, a small Eskimo village at the headwaters of the John River, the next day.

John lashed four-foot willow extensions to the tent poles to make them reach the bottom of the drifts. He stretched his canvas sled tarp over the tent to keep the wet heavy snow from building up on the tent during the night. At 30° above, the willow fire gave plenty of heat and all our gear got dried out. With the storm blustering outside, we were snug and warm.

The next morning three to four feet of snow had accumulated. The dogs wallowed along the snowshoe track. The wet snow globbed on underneath the sled, pulling it off into the deep snow. I continually cleaned out the snow, and the sled pulled easier for a short 50 feet.

In the blowing snow, all we could see were occasional willows poking up above the drifts and some dark rocks blown clear on the steep walls of the pass. Our map told us we were in the Valley of the Precipices, and we sensed the rugged slopes on either side of us. The map also showed only 20 miles of uphill to the crest of the pass, but we still were climbing on the third day of snowshoeing.

We stopped for lunch, and I unpacked the lunch bag and poured hot water in the vacuum bottle cups. Just as John sat down on the sled the clouds parted and we could see ahead for several miles. John recognized the opportunity and sprinted — if it's

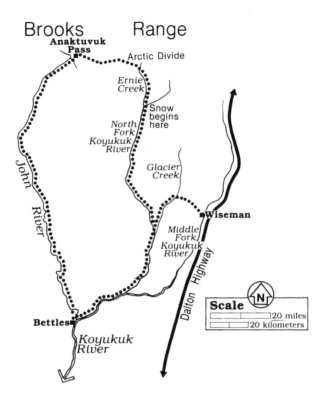

possible to sprint on snowshoes in four feet of new snow — to a
high ridge. The Arctic was kind to give us this break in the clouds.
The view showed we were almost to the top. A turn to the left
would lead us down into the Anaktuvuk River valley.

I threw the lunch back in my sled bag and carefully poured the
precious hot water back in the vacuum bottles. I snowshoed along
in John's tracks and called the dogs to follow. Suddenly the dogs
were overtaking me. We were going downhill!

About three miles farther down the snow was less deep and the
dogs could go ahead. We left the creek bottom and stayed up on
the exposed ridge, where the wind was doing its work. A stand
of dark willows moved in front of us. Branches turned into antlers,
and when the wind gave them our scent, the band of 16 caribou
sprang off across the tundra. They held their heads up stiffly and
their noses kept track of us as they bounded several miles in a
few minutes.

A few of the dogs saw them and shifted into chasing gear. The
rest of the team picked up their fresh scent when we crossed their
tracks, and a frenzied sniffing surge lasted for about a half-mile.

Throughout the afternoon we encountered bands of caribou, and the dogs always strained and zoomed in pursuit.

As the sky slowly cleared the temperature dropped. Near-vertical walls of mountain materialized out of the blowing snow on either side of us. The walls were a dark contrast to the bright whiteness that was everywhere else. They looked as if the glacier that had scoured them had just disappeared.

The three-mile-wide valley was open and clean, windy and white. The tundra rolled out gently, sparkling back to the sun. Small patches of low vegetation and tufts of tussocks exposed by the wind hinted at the tundra's summer face. Abandoned caribou antlers created little snowdrifts in their lee as they weathered in the wind, graceful monuments to the great herds that had migrated through the valley in the past.

I wondered how long the antlers took to return to the soil, to be broken down by the bright lichens and gnawed away by little creatures. The Nunamiut Eskimos living at Anaktuvuk Pass had probably killed most of these caribou, but I wondered if some of the oldest antlers were left from earlier days, before 1950 when the permanent village was established. This central area of the Brooks Range was the territory of the nomadic bands of Nunamiut. Long before the first Russian fur traders stepped ashore on Alaskan shores these Eskimos were waiting for the caribou to migrate up this valley.

As my sled slipped over the tundra, I was overwhelmed by a closeness to a more primitive time. My belly was full, yet I sensed what it was to squint out over the hills, searching for a caribou that would feed my family and provide a thick skin for clothing. How strong those people were to survive in this awesome country! How many had starved to death when the caribou didn't come in time?

About noon we eased over a hill, and the village of Anaktuvuk Pass bloomed on the tundra before us. Brightly painted plywood prefabs hid the few remaining sod houses. Power poles lined the streets, intersecting the low profile of the village. John's wide eyes hardly recognized the place.

We visited John's friends and heard snatches of news covering the past 10 years. The village had undergone many changes. The people seemed to welcome the modernization. Each home had a large color TV offering 24-hour cable selections. The sets were always turned on, often with the sound off, so conversations could be heard. CB radios were also turned on in every house. People liked to keep up on local gossip. When someone traveled out of the village on a snow machine, the CB was valuable in case of emergencies.

Caribou hides hung on drying racks outside nearly every house. Several new snow machines were parked in front. There was a combination of old and new, and an overriding feeling of prosperity. The people were busy and healthy. Most important, they radiated that unique Eskimo way of smiling at the world, of taking each day at a time, enjoying the present. More changes would come to Anaktuvuk, but it seemed these people had the depth and stability to take it all in stride. John and I planned to return in 10 more years and see the changes.

The south wind continued to blow. The villagers were waiting for the north wind to clear away the snow. Impatient trappers who traveled by snow machine kept trying to open their trails, but the soft deep snow turned them back. No one in the village used dogs anymore. We joked with several trappers, suggesting that they break trail for their machines with snowshoes. This made a great joke, but the men agreed it was the only way they could move until the wind blew.

We had planned to stay in Anaktuvuk for several days. Considering the continuing slow conditions we knew we must keep going if we wanted our supplies to carry us to Bettles, some 170 miles to the south. Raymond Paneak, our host for the night, had our frozen food safe in his storage tent. The rest of our dog food waited at the post office. The next morning we packed up, said our good-bys, and headed down the John River.

The sun was breaking through for the first time in five days, but the wind was roaring into our faces from the south. Snow machines were buzzing out the trails in all directions from town. Everyone was taking advantage of the break in the clouds.

During our second day traveling down the John River the wind switched and chased us from the north. It chased with a fury, and we were grateful it came at our backs. The snow covering the ice was whisked downriver, and we sailed along at a good clip. The temperature was 12° above, but the 30-mile-per-hour wind chill factor forced us into all our winter gear again.

John stood sideways to the wind for a moment, and one of his soft contact lenses was blown clean out of his eye! Reluctantly he put on his frosty glasses for the rest of the trip.

As we continued south, downstream, the willow thickets became more substantial. We watched for the first cottonwoods, the first spruce, the first birch, and finally the first aspen. With each new species the forest marked the diminishing effects of the cold north wind. We were still in the Arctic, but a milder, more gentle Arctic.

We reached Bettles on the seventh night after leaving Anaktuvuk. Both of us had come down with the flu, on two different days, and the layovers ate up the dog food. We had only a half-night's feeding left in our sleds, so we dipped into our fresh supplies which Ray Bane had picked up at the Bettles post office. Ray had lived in the North for many years. Presently he worked for the National Park Service, coordinating subsistence uses in the National Interest lands. His insights into the conflicting uses of the land were based on a first-hand understanding of subsistence needs and a vision of the future. Ray's dedication and sincerity were impressive. He spoke bureaucratic jargon, but he was in touch with the land and the people.

The next day we left Bettles, heading northeast toward Wiseman on the old mail trail that Olaus and Mardy Murie had followed and described in Mardy's wonderful book, *Two in The Far North*. The north fork valley had not changed much since their trip. The new national park status meant protection in the future, although the designation would surely bring thousands of visitors.

The next valley to the east, the middle fork of the Koyukuk, was a different story. The trans-Alaska oil pipeline snaked its way down that valley, gleaming dully as it slithered underground and up again. An endless stream of huge trucks ground up the haul road, dumped their loads at Prudhoe Bay, and returned south, taking 32 hours for a round trip. The sounds of change in that valley seemed to echo into every other drainage in Alaska.

But back in the north fork our dog trail was clean and quiet. The snowy river represented "the freshness, the freedom, the farness," that Robert Service had told me about 17 years earlier. As we made our way back to Wiseman, I tried to define those words with my own meaning.

"The freshness" was celebrating each day as a precious gift. The chores, the daily routine and the dog team adventures all were necessary parts evolving into a satisfying whole.

"The freedom" was the decision to take my time; to make the days, the seasons, the years full of meaning. Understanding the country from the back of a dog sled gave me a comfortable feeling of being at home in the wilderness.

"The farness" was the great Alaskan heartland; the meandering rivers draining the rolling foothills that stretched up to the high mountain passes. Traveling quietly through that vast country filled me with respect and challenged me to live up to the land's high standards, to "grow bigger with the bigness of the whole."

So now you have listened to my heart and you know where my dreams take me. Each spring when the clearest blue sky calls and the sun arcs a little higher each day, my path will lead out to where there is no trail. Lucky stars, my good dogs and John's warm companionship have allowed me to know the wonders of that trail. These pages are my attempt to share those wonders with you and to encourage you to listen to your own heart and follow your own trail. You don't even need a dog team.